FOR INCLUDED WITH THE END IN MIND

Included with The End in Mind is a well-written and well-researched book that provides professionals and parents with detailed concepts that are necessary for bridging inclusive educational practices for youth with disabilities. Amy's personal examples are superbly woven into the fabric of each chapter. This is a must-read book for your library.

Cindi Nixon, Associate Professor, Francis Marion University, South Carolina

---

Amy draws from diverse professional and personal experiences to create a resource that is hopeful as it is practical. This is a rich and insightful resource that draws from powerful professional and personal experiences. It clearly illustrates the impact of empowerment and collaboration. This book illuminates the path towards effective transition and brighter futures.

Sean Roy, Co-Director, PACER's National Parent Center on Transition and Employment, Minneapolis

---

Bravo! This should be required reading for college level education classes, especially for secondary special education and school leadership. So much can be learned about modernizing services systemically as well as strategies to improve systems and classrooms. This content has inherent balance of the theoretical and the practical. Amy's writing is attention getting, genuine, sincere, based on experience, and believable. There are gems to be had by all with exceptional quotes and other information that will give professionals many 'A-ha!' moments, as well as food for thought and discussion.

Monica Quann, Transition Coordinator, New Castle County Vocational Technical School District, Delaware

---

A must read for educators who want to make a difference for all of their students. Pleet–Odle provides thoughtful reflections on systematic inclusion practices that are evidenced-based, concrete and proven in the classroom. The author's broad experience in the field and relevant stories are invaluable lessons to share.

Steven H. Godowsky, Ed.D., Secretary of Education, Delaware Department of Education

ADVANCE PRAISE **FOR INCLUDED WITH THE END IN MIND**

Dr. Pleet-Odle has a first-hand perspective of the evolution of transition services in the United States. From teacher, then parent, college professor to finally an educational consultant, Amy has witnessed the best of the best to the worst of the worst. She shares her journey in an easy-to-read narrative that points to the heart of needed change.

James P. Heiden, PhD, Superintendent, School District of Cudahy, Wisconsin

---

They say timing is everything—and the time could not be more perfect for this book. Amy Pleet-Odle has that marvelous combination of the practitioner and observer. She understands that education is indeed a delicate balance of art and science, compassion and action. In this book she shares what she has discovered—ALL students—those with a seemingly effortless gift for comprehending the most abstract of concepts and those who struggle mightily to grasp even the most basic material—have the same need for compassionate and imaginative teachers who believe that every child can achieve important milestones if given the right tools and teachers and leaders who will recognize and appreciate them as unique individuals with great potential to succeed.

George P. Tilson, Ed.D., Founder and Senior Associate, Tilson & Diaz Solutions, Inc. Instructor, University of Kansas, Department of Special Education

---

Ultimately, educators will be judged not on their good intentions, but on how well they create opportunities and outcomes for students. Dr. Pleet-Odle crafts a fully comprehensive guide for making Inclusion come alive in schools. We walk away with not only one great idea after another, but with an understanding of how to strategically make our worthy vision of inclusion thrive amidst the realities of a modern school.

David Jezyk, Supervisor of Exceptional Children and Title One Programs, New Castle County Vocational Technical School District, Delaware

INCLUDED WITH THE END IN MIND

Integrating Efforts to Improve
Outcomes for Youth with Disabilities

INCLUDED WITH THE END IN MIND

*Integrating Efforts
to Improve Outcomes
for Youth with Disabilities*

AMY M. **PLEET-ODLE**

INCLUDED WITH THE END IN MIND

Integrating Efforts to Improve Outcomes for Youth with Disabilities

ACKNOWLEDGMENTS

This book is an expression of my heart that has been nurtured through navigating the learning path with wise friends and colleagues over the years too numerous to mention here.

I appreciate mentoring and collaborative learning from educators who were there for me throughout the many twists and turns of my career. I will start with those who were there when I began my career: Scotty Maxwell, my first department chair and mentor, and fellow Baltimore County Public Schools professionals, Cindi Amirault, Marsye Kaplan, Vicky Ciulla, Rosemary Rappa, Jerry Malin, and Nancy Hesselbein. I would also like to acknowledge Art and Susan Nierenberg, Margaret Glenn, Bev Vargo, Odette Levac, Erica Perry, David Tartaglia, and Suzanne Ross from the Breakthrough Disability learning community.

I am grateful for the following colleagues in the transition community: Dorothy Allison, Sheldon Meyers, Ginger Holliway, Berenda Riedl, Dennis Snyder, Colleen Gauruder, Peggy Hayeslip, George Tilson, Joyce Serio, Tom Barkley, Rich Luecking, Kris Webb, Mike Wehmeyer, Sharon DeFur, Jim Heiden, Mary Morningstar, Catherine Fowler, David Test, Joy Ivester, Jim Martin, Donna Wandry, Meg Grigal, Joanne Cashman, Mary Morningstar, Cindi Nixon, Lynda West, Ruth Brodsky, Carol Kochhar-Bryant, Jane Razeghi, Dawn Rowe, Christy Stuart, and Monica Simonson.

I am thankful for opportunities to learn from the following educational leaders: Carol Quirk, Dorie Flynn, Louise Supnick, Beverly German, Maya Kalyanpur, Shelley Rouser, Darren Guido, Sharon Brittingham, Jackie Wilson, Steven Godowsky, Lisa Lawson, Rachel Burwell, Gene Montano, and Joyce Denman; and family engagement leaders Joyce Epstein, Karen Mapp, Sean Roy, Mona Freedman, Michele Brooks, Patricia Spradley, and Marta Bentham.

I cherish the consultation brainstorming time I spent with Cathy Raggio, Laura Eisenman, Monica Quann, Terri Villa, Michele Savage, Heather Austin, Kelley Brake, Dave Jezyk, Deanna Hess, Vickie Robinson, and Karen Clark.

I must also thank my writing coach, Allison Nappi, who helped me discover how to give voice to my inner passion, and Leah Lakins, my copy editor, who helped bring this book to the finish line.

And finally I give thanks to my husband, Robert, who has listened to ideas for these chapters on many dog walks, my sisters who have accepted that I'll never fully retire, and my seven children who taught me countless lessons about persistence and possibilities in life. Ultimately, I'm grateful for all those who never stopped believing in me, even when I lingered in my garden. You've taught me that the most important thing in life is friends who can see possibilities.

DEDICATION

I dedicate this book and the determination that made it possible to my mother, Dorothy Ramsdill Thomas. Responsibility was instilled in her early on the family dairy farm in upstate New York. My three siblings and I grew up hearing about our mother milking cows and gathering eggs before dawn so she could ride the milk wagon into town for school. We knew that childhood polio left her with backaches and a lift in one shoe. But we knew she was luckier than many children who died or were left paralyzed. We begged to hear the story of our Dad, who was a local town boy and a son of a minister, asking to walk her home after school, not realizing it would be over five miles.

Like most children, we took our parents for granted. My mother didn't continue working as an executive secretary after we were born. Money may have been tight, but we didn't know it. Our parents gave up things that could have made their lives more enjoyable so that we could have rich lives that included scouting, attending Sunday school, singing in the church choir, playing sports, and enjoying piano and dance lessons. We travelled to historic sites on family vacations. I still sigh and roll my eyes at museum displays of bullets.

The remarkable part of my mother's life was invisible to us. The dining room table was often littered with some project. We never asked what she was working on, but years later her finished pieces came back to us. When Mom passed at age 83, my sisters and I were speechless when the church was packed during her funeral. I had lived out of state for 20 years, so I only recognized a few people. There were women there who told us that Mom had trained all the Girl Scout leaders in Delaware. They came to salute her leadership.

Others came because Mom had organized an ecumenical group, called Fish, to support neighbors in need, inviting members of diverse denominations. They told us that by the time they came to a meeting, Mom already had a plan to have teams of volunteers tackling various community needs. Some prepared home cooked meals and delivered to people who were shut-ins, similar to Meals on Wheels that was starting in Philadelphia. She laundered donated clothing for families who were down on their luck. Decades before internet searches, she had made phone calls and assembled information about agencies that would help in case of a house fire, domestic abuse, alcoholism, death without insurance, or foster care. She hand-typed a copy of her directory for anyone who asked. She even typed one for the governor. Guests reminisced about the radio interview on her groundbreaking work that would later be coordinated by social services. But we thought that Mom didn't work.

By hearing these stories, I understood my drive to make a difference. I carry my mother in my heart and my bones. She would be proud of my work. I hope it will continue her commitment to make a difference in the world. Love you, Mom.

FOREWORD

For over 30 years, educators have struggled, preached, researched, and described methods to include students with disabilities. Journals such as *Inclusion* published by the American Association for Intellectual and Developmental Disabilities, and *Research and Practice for People with Severe Disabilities* published by TASH, regularly publish articles about what works in inclusive schools. There are numerous books about inclusive education. Some focus on instructional practices, others on school reform, and others on specific, research-based methods to teach academic, social-behavioral, or communication skills.

So what makes this book different? The difference is that *Included with The End in Mind* is a personal and professional journey that does not preach or approach inclusion as an odious task. Instead, it describes the realities that are experienced every day by educators, administrators, and parents as opportunities to move toward a more inclusive approach to teach all students.

Early research and literature on how to teach students with disabilities focused on specific instructional strategies taught in isolation or in special education classrooms apart from the educational life experienced by their non-disabled peers. It did not assume that students with disabilities would experience a variety of instructional approaches used by different general education teachers, which vary by geography and also continuously change over time. It also did not assume that there were actual social and learning opportunities in general education.

Since then, as research has repeatedly demonstrated the benefits of teaching students with disabilities in general education settings, and as professional literature describes organizational and academic approaches to successfully include all students, there has been a global movement toward inclusive education. Consequently, we are at a point in time where we must assume that all learners belong in the school and classroom they would attend if they were not disabled. We must assume that all of the adults in a school are responsible for all students in the building. We assume that they will work together collaboratively for each and every child's success. We must assume that parents are important partners in educational planning. We assume that the information and ideas that they bring to discussions will contribute to school decisions. As professionals we need to understand the contributions of various disabilities to the learning process and support a culture of belonging among all the students in our care.

In this book, Dr. Amy Pleet-Odle puts inclusive education in the context of the wide variety of demands on our schools, uses research findings as the back drop for her recommendations, and provides a framework for instructional planning that focuses on individual and personalized student learning. It is a unique view, not from one who only observes or consults with others who do the work, but from one who lives and has lived the inclusive education experience. With this book, educators will find a friend and a resource.

Carol Quirk, Ed.D., Executive Director
Maryland Coalition for Inclusive Education

MY CAREER EVOLUTION

I am not a teacher, but an awakener.
ROBERT FROST

The passion for teaching that began for me in childhood has persisted for nearly five decades. My career path resembles the trajectory of a billiard ball that deflects off other balls and the rails. There have been seven such deflections in my career, but through it all, my focus has been on discovering and creating more effective ways to reach struggling students.

I created a graphic organizer as I was writing each chapter to keep myself organized. Then I decided I should practice what I preach and provide you, my reader, the scaffolding to digest my key points. I've included a graphic organizer of the content within each chapter. I designed a variety of organizers to model that there isn't one right way to tame complex material. Figure I.1 shows an organizer that represents my career evolution.

Figure I.1

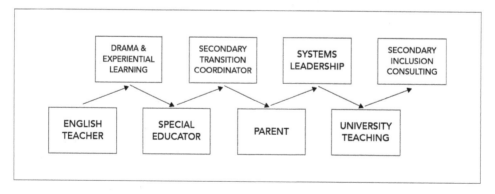

I started my career as a 7th-grade English teacher. I employed the traditional sage-on-the-stage methods that I knew. Was there any other way to teach? This was before we had a special education law, so there was a broad range of abilities and skills in my classroom. I stayed up late at night worrying about challenging the brightest students and inspiring the slowest of my students.

Pathway 1: Incorporating Drama and Experiential Learning

My first pathway came when I discovered the equalizing power of drama and experiential learning. Both of these methods engage students' hearts and imaginations in learning content and go way beyond memorized facts and vocabulary. My heart aches whenever I walk into a classroom today and spot students with their heads down. When I hear teachers complain that their students won't pay attention, I itch to model more creative ways to put student learning at the heart of classroom activities. I believe that engagement is the antidote for teacher burnout and student dropout.

Pathway 2: Working With the Education of the Handicapped Act of 1975

The passage of the *Education of the Handicapped Act of 1975* brought my second pathway. I was intrigued that year by a 7th-grade student who wrote like a 1st-grader. Dale was an active leader in discussions about character motivation, and he often volunteered to dramatize background context and interpret passages that were read aloud. He often suggested parallel patterns in current events. Yet, he would do anything to avoid literacy tasks with emergency trips to the boys' room, the nurse, the guidance counselor, and, if all else failed, the pencil sharpener. He was a puzzle to me. How could such a bright young man have so much difficulty with reading and writing?

Within one week of hearing about this new law and the new disability category called learning disabilities, I referred Dale to the special education team and learned first hand about child-find procedures. In the end, Dale was still in my class, but he was now eligible to visit the resource room for extra help with his reading and writing. Because of Dale, I became a special educator.

I understand teachers' drive to be the catalyst for bringing success to struggling students. In those days we placed students with disabilities into self-contained and resource classrooms to give them the support they needed. I started a middle school program and later chaired a large special education department and led IEP team meetings. I saw the significant impact I could have when I provided a context for disability acceptance at team meetings for parents, teachers, and most of all, students.

Dale and other students visited me after graduating, full of heart wrenching stories of college failure, unfair bosses, and abandoned jobs. Their employers didn't give them the same pat on the back encouragement as teachers. There was no praise when they completed their expected tasks—only criticism when they did something wrong. I would hear my former students say things like, "He can't talk to me like that. So I quit." To avoid the stigma of the special education room, they didn't seek disability service offices on campus. They would say, "I'm not in special ed anymore!" But without accommodations and knowledge of the scaffolding I had provided to them, they didn't pass their classes. I felt that I had let them down by only thinking about their short-term success. Educational coddling prevented these students from building critical inner resources.

Pathway 3: Becoming a Transition Specialist

Secondary transition was my third pathway where I served seven local middle and high schools. My job description said I would support students and their families to use vocational assessments to make career choices and select programs and activities during high school and beyond to prepare them for successful outcomes. But my secret mission was to give teachers strategies they could use in the classroom to support student awareness of their own disabilities and self-advocacy skills. I met with employers, vocational rehabilitation counselors, and college disability support personnel to learn more about their experiences. I would then relay this information to middle and high school teachers. I organized workshops to inform families about transition options and provided checklists they could use to guide their parenting.

Pathway 4: Being the Parent on the Other Side of the Table

My fourth pathway came from my personal life. Both my children were eventually identified as having disabilities, so I sat at many IEP conference tables. I was often confused about my role. For years, I participated in IEP meetings as a general educator, special educator, transition coordinator, and team leader. But, as the parent, I was expected to passively follow the lead of the professionals on the team. When I proposed services or recommended other annual goals, I felt the tremors of fear in my stomach. I guess Eleanor Roosevelt was right when she said, "A woman is like a tea bag. You never know how strong she is until she gets in hot water." I'm still second guessing whether I was strong enough.

In too many teams there was a climate of "us versus them," with parents holding the burden of being "them." I was dismayed to reflect on all the ways I had contributed to those conditions as a professional, and I was determined for my future to help build partnerships. Most of my publications and national presentations focused on professional strategies to support families as they become contributing partners. I was especially passionate about empowering their young adults to develop self-determination skills.

Pathway 5: Expanding My Leadership

Out of a commitment to transform education with the end in mind, I sought out system leadership positions, my fifth pathway. I was mentored at the time by Art Nierenberg of Breakthrough Disability and gaining skills in the art of coaching for empowerment. I immersed myself in doctoral studies, which was not easy as a divorced working mother. My two doctoral internships broadened my perspectives. I spearheaded the creation of the Maryland Transition Website and commuted to the U.S. Office of Special Education in Washington, DC to categorize the federally funded special education leadership fellowships.

When the special education reauthorization instituted new transition requirements in 1997, I was the Maryland Department of Education Transition Specialist. My horizons expanded from collaboration opportunities with transition specialists in other states. Together, we designed ways to infuse vital transition practices into the heart of school procedures.

With the Secretary of the Department of Disabilities, I co-chaired the Maryland Interagency Transition Council and worked passionately on issues like drop-outs, incarcerated youth, interagency collaboration, career preparation, and family engagement. I was learning what it took to create systems where adults and youth could work together. However, change wasn't happening fast enough on the front line.

Pathway 6: Leading the Next Generation

My sixth pathway occurred when I took the position of Special Education Graduate Director at Towson University in Maryland. I was appointed to create a graduate special education program. I knew what was missing in my own teacher preparation. New teachers needed models of empowerment and engaging learning activities. They needed to know how the pieces fit together to prepare students ultimately for a life of independence and self-sufficiency. They needed experience in their role as a coach in the process. Most of all, these teachers needed to see themselves as creative problem solvers.

As I interviewed each new candidate, I was reminded repeatedly about the bright-eyed optimism of men and women entering the profession. I believe all teachers are profoundly called to make a difference. Supervising my graduate students during their final semester internship, I was immersed again in the complex world of a classroom. I felt their stressors of proctoring state exams, learning curricular pacing guides, assessing their students' needs, and struggling within systems that didn't always support them. But I was thrilled my interns used creative, engaging approaches from their coursework. At their core, they were learners and experimenters who were eager for new ideas and open for coaching.

Pathway 7: Bringing it All Together

Pathway number seven has combined all my previous experiences as a consultant on school transformation through the University of Delaware and then in private practice. Secondary schools seek outside support as they strive to successfully integrate special education students from self-contained classes into inclusive settings. I appreciate district leaders and principals who are open to rethinking strategic systems of support. I provide professional development and coaching to general and special educators related to inclusive instructional approaches and family engagement. With each interaction, my commitment is to empower practitioners to think systematically. I encourage professionals to keep the end in mind by targeting critical post-school skills as they design instruction and support student self-efficacy.

I expanded my understanding of systems change as a certified trainer for Learning Focused Solutions, a FIT assessor for the SWIFT Center at the University of Kansas, and content expert at the National Technical Assistance Center for Transition's Capacity Building Institute. All three organizations use a systems approach to expanding knowledge and skills of teachers and leaders. They also use well-delineated frameworks to guide team strategic planning, implementation, and ongoing improvement.

I decided to write this book out of a profound commitment to transform educational practice. I have reached that point in my life and career where it all makes sense. I can see how the pieces fit into a system. More importantly, I see the dangers of a fragmented approach to systems change. This book presents my personal and professional journey, combining real anecdotes with research findings and strategies that work. My intention is that you will come away with new insights into your own circumstances, whether you are a teacher, an administrator, a parent, a district leader, or a community partner. As my mentor, Arthur Nierenberg, used to say, "There are no answers here." I can't give you answers to your dilemmas, but I have learned many of the questions to ask. I have organized the key professional competencies that served as foundation for discovering your own answers to difficult questions. Together we can create the context so that when students with disabilities walk across the stage, their public schooling end will be just the beginning.

CHAPTER ONE

TRANSITION: THE END AND THE BEGINNING

Education is the power to think clearly, the power to act well in the world's work, and the power to appreciate life.
BRIGHAM YOUNG

When I became a transition coordinator, I felt as though I had landed on my home base. At last I had a chance to do something that would truly make a difference. My job description was a list of duties from special education law stating I was responsible for coordinating activities to prepare youth with disabilities to successfully transition into adult settings, including employment, further education, and community living. But in my heart, this job was so much more.

Like every transition coordinator I've met, I spend untold hours and personal creative energy designing practices that would change the trajectory of youth with special needs. I witnessed first hand how one student, Gregory, functioned at his job and realized that he had no idea how he learned new procedures. His caring teachers had provided needed supports without partnering with him. As a teacher, I had done the same things—and missed an opportunity. It became clear to me that the whole team needed to be aligned on ways to prepare him for self-reliance if we wanted to improve his outcomes. Over the last 30 years, my resolve for this purpose has been strengthened at national transition conferences by the camaraderie and passion of like-minded individuals.

A few years ago, I attended two state conferences in the same week, one focused on transition and the other on inclusion. I noticed that transition was never mentioned at the inclusion conference and transition sessions never mentioned opportunities for student growth through inclusive practices. I also observed that there were very few people who attended both conferences.

We operate as though these are totally separate initiatives. But are they? In the sea of multiple improvement efforts that bombard schools, professionals think of inclusion and transition as separate disciplines. These efforts are often not integrated into the whole secondary experience for these students. Yet, inclusion and transition both target the same outcome—preparing students to be successful in a post-school world.

In many places, complying with transition requirements is provided by a lone transition coordinator without much awareness or buy-in from other team members. When I was a district transition coordinator, team leaders often asked me to meet with the student and family separately after the IEP meeting to discuss transition issues and options. They were dubious when I protested that transition discussions were for the whole team and that the student's post-school goals should drive our IEP planning.

Today, when leading a workshop focused on inclusive practices, teachers are surprised when I begin by talking about transition planning and outcomes. Often someone raises a hand to tell me, "We don't deal with transition. We have a transition coordinator to handle all that." Transition is not separate. Students' preparation for adult life is the targeted outcome for effective inclusive practices.

This book is written for folks like me who are concerned about secondary education. We feel there must be a better way to reach all youth and to help them prepare for a world that is rapidly changing. We look at the shifts in cultural and economic climate and see how we were taught will not work for students graduating from our schools today, especially those students with compounding problems related to having a disability.

The questions we must raise and the answers we will seek arise from multiple sources. I bring nearly five decades of experience to this quest. Along the way, I have gained insight and clarifying wisdom from myriad experiences. First, teaching English and then special education, I lived the frustrations of juggling competing priorities. As a parent, I witnessed how often impersonal school practices disenfranchised my engagement. As a transition coordinator in a district and at a state department, I grappled with scaling up approaches to prepare students to exit public school ready to enter adult settings. As a university professor, I experimented with activities that would foster teacher candidates' problem-solving skills, combining research with trust in their own professional judgment. And now, as a secondary inclusion consultant, I partner with school administrators and faculty to improve effectiveness of our service delivery systems. Having worked from different perspectives, I can see that we are not pulling together.

More than ever, I see that schools and our society are buffeted by polarizing competing priorities. Teachers and school leaders are bombarded with multiple approaches that separately bring solutions, but educators are overwhelmed by this fragmented approach. We will not truly transform our educational systems if we focus separately on each component puzzle piece. I agree with Michael Fullan in *The Six Secrets of Change* (2008) when he said, "A fragmented approach is a barrier to change."

When I met my husband, a systems engineer, five years ago, I did not anticipate the way he would influence my thinking. His curious questions spurred thoughtful conversations about how all the parts fit together in schools. The schematic models he designs in his work inspired me to experiment with graphic representations of an integrated system. From discussions with him, I conceptualized the pieces of the puzzle we call education. I learned to value each piece, including the cultural climate, stakeholder roles, infrastructure, instructional methodology, leadership, student empowerment, and family and community engagement.

Education is a system dependent on all the parts. Each stakeholder, including all students, teachers, staff, administrators, district leaders, families, and the community has a valued contribution to make. Any strategic plan must take into account each group's roles, valued resources, and skill sets. Each member of the team must have an appreciation of the grand interconnectedness in education. The intent of this book is to take you on a journey to see how all the parts contribute to one system and empower you to transform your own schools.

The Legal Requirements of Secondary Transition

I've called this book *Included with The End in Mind* so that we can set our sights on that point when students with disabilities exit from secondary school. For students with disabilities, transition from secondary education to post-school settings is the end and the beginning. After 13 or more years, their formal public education will come to an end. Their services under special education law will also end when they exit high school, regardless of whether they leave with a high school diploma, a special education certificate, or as a dropout. At the same time, they will begin their adult lives. Will they be ready?

In 1997, the reauthorized *Individuals with Disabilities Education Act (IDEA)* first introduced transition requirements to ease the passage from special education procedures and protections into an often disjointed and confusing array of supports. I had just been hired as the transition specialist for the Maryland State Department of Education. My phone started ringing. Special education directors across the state wanted to know what they needed to do. I was an experienced transition coordinator and was working on my doctorate with a focus on secondary special education transition. However, we didn't know yet what the requirements would mean in practice. Luckily, I could collaborate with the federally funded Maryland Transition Initiative grant leaders and with my counterparts in the adult systems of vocational rehabilitation, developmental disabilities, and mental health.

Our team attended U.S. Office of Special Education (OSEP) briefings on the law's new requirements at transition institutes in Washington, DC. Leaders and researchers with experience implementing transition practices and programs all over the country were there. We could share initiatives from Maryland and hear what was happening in other locations. As shown in Figure 1.1, we built on each other's efforts to expand our practices under the rallying cry to improve outcomes for youth with disabilities. Many of those visionary leaders became my friends. Nearly 20 years later, we continue to be inspired by each other's drive for improvement at the Division on Career Development and Transition international conferences.

Figure 1.1

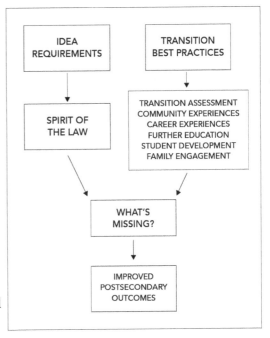

Today, special education operates under 2004 IDEA revisions. As in previous versions of the law, all students who qualify for special education services have an annual plan called an Individualized Education Program (IEP). The IEP is developed by a multidisciplinary team including at least one of the child's general education teachers, a special educator, a team leader or administrator, the child's parents, and any specialists (e.g., guidance counselor, psychologist, speech therapist, career technology teacher or nurse) who can contribute relevant information.

When the student becomes transition age, 16 in IDEA, earlier in some states, the IEP must also include the following transition components:

- **Age-appropriate transition assessments:** This section outlines the formal and informal methods for gathering information to help plan the youth's future (e.g., career interests, present skills, aptitudes, work behaviors, preferences, and weaknesses).

- **Measurable postsecondary goals:** This section provides the student's goals for further education, employment, and (if appropriate) independent living arrangements, stating intended outcomes for the youth one year after graduation.

- **Transition services and supports:** This section lists transition services the school, family, and related services will provide to enable the student to reach his goals.

- **Secondary school course of study:** This section outlines the school courses and programs through graduation that will prepare the student to reach her postsecondary goals.

- **Annual goals:** This section includes what the student and school team will focus on during the coming year related to the student's transition needs.

- **Invitation:** This is a document that shows that the student, family, and relevant agency personnel (if any) have been invited to the IEP meeting (U.S. Department of Special Education Policy, 2012, May).

Upholding the Spirit of the Law

Originally, when OSEP staff monitored states, they focused on compliance with specific regulations. I experienced the anxiety of an OSEP audit in 1999 when I was the state transition specialist. After reviewing IEP files during the day, OSEP personnel would often make visits to schools. They met with groups of parents to gather information about complaints. In the end, most of their evaluative report was created from their file review. It's understandable that we used the same method to evaluate the districts and schools across our state.

Advocates protested that there was little correlation between completing IEP paperwork accurately and producing strong youth outcomes. IDEA 2004 had expanded the purpose of special education as follows:

> To ensure that all children with disabilities have available to them a free appropriate public education that emphasizes special education and related services designed to meet their unique needs and prepare them for further education, employment, and independent living.

On a grand scale, this purpose was not being fulfilled. Advocates pointed to the disturbing results of the second federally funded National Longitudinal Transition Study of Special Education Students (NLTS2). The NLTS2 had collected data from 2000–2010 with a representative sample of 11,000 students with disabilities across the country. Research analysts at the Institute of Education Sciences (2011) reported post-school outcomes of these youth. Here are some of the findings three to five years after they left high school as compared with the first NLTS of 8,000 students (Blackorby & Wagner, 1996):

- A slight rise in some type of employment, now 60%, compared with 55% in 1993, but most youth had part time or minimum wage jobs.
- An increased percentage of youth with disabilities who had enrolled at some time in postsecondary education (60% as compared with 27% in 1993), but less than one-third disclosed their disability and only 40% of those who attended completed their degree or certificate.
- The number of youth with disabilities who were arrested (32%). Shockingly, 60% of youth with emotional disturbance reported being arrested. Comparison with prior data wasn't possible since this question wasn't included in the earlier study.

The intent of special education services is to prepare every student with disabilities for success in adult life. Yet, these studies indicated that we were making minimal progress. The gap between students with and without disabilities was not closing. The graduation rate in 2013 was 81% for the general population as compared with 62% for students with disabilities. These findings called professionals to closely examine our practices to see what was missing.

In response to these studies and other indicators, OSEP (U.S. Office of Special Education Policy, 2012, May) announced a shift in their monitoring policy from verifying compliance in paperwork to a result-driven accountability system. Within their announcement, they made the following statements:

- The educational outcomes of America's children and youth with disabilities have not improved as much as expected, despite significant federal efforts to close achievement gaps.

- An emphasis on compliance over results in special education fails to acknowledge those states where children with disabilities are achieving and being prepared for a range of college and career options appropriate to their individual needs and preferences.

This announcement refocused the intent of special education services on improving post-school outcomes for youth with disabilities. The spirit of the law is to keep the end in mind as we provide special education services. The 2013 OSEP annual report charged states to analyze the quality and effectiveness of their services. We still have some work to do, but our path forward is clear.

Understanding Transition Practices

Since 1984, I have been deeply immersed in professional communities of practice to improve the provision of transition services. As a district transition coordinator, I brainstormed frequently with other transition practitioners in schools and community agencies. As the transition specialist at the Maryland Department of Education, I conducted interactive think tank sessions with transition personnel across the state. For six years, I cochaired the Maryland Interagency Transition Council, leading the task force that created the state transition website. I served two terms on the national board of the Division on Career Development and Transition, attending and presenting at local and national conferences. I co-authored several publications and served on the editorial board reviewing research articles. Throughout all these activities, I kept asking myself, "These initiatives are so exciting. Why aren't we seeing improved results on a large scale?"

There were locations across the country (and some that I helped develop in Maryland and Delaware) where professionals had established amazing programs. Students were involved in job shadowing, career mentoring, college experiences, and paid employment. Transition professionals developed collaborative relationships with college disability services and with employers. It troubled me that these isolated programs contributed to improved outcomes for their youth, but other locations seldom replicated their practices. Worse, they were always struggling to keep their funding.

The partnership program between St. Mary's Public Schools and the College of Southern Maryland (CSM) is a good example. Their Self-Discovery Through College Connections program targets students with mental health disabilities who are at risk for dropping out. These high school students are identified to participate in 10 afternoon sessions each semester on the CSM campus that are designed to give them early college experiences. Their sessions cover topics such as personal power and values, self-esteem, trust and leadership, anger management, affording college, and workplace etiquette. In addition, these youths have a CSM identification card giving them rights and benefits as a college student. After six years, 100% of the nearly 100 students in this program graduated with a high school diploma and some even enrolled in college. These results are astounding, but to my knowledge the program has not been replicated.

Including Evidence-Based Transition Practices

Kohler's Taxonomy for Transition Programming (1996), revised in 2016, has endured as a useful organizational model for the following five key components of transition:

1. **Student-focused planning:** Using the IEP process to put students at the center of short- and long-term planning for their futures, including resources and supports identified in their transition assessments.

2. **Student development:** Providing supports targeting student growth in academic, life, social, and emotional skills, as well as employment and occupational competencies, based on a range of assessments and embedded in the instructional context.

3. **Interagency collaboration:** Building a coordinated and collaborative system of services and supports between educators, disability service providers, families, and consumers.

4. **Family engagement:** Involving, preparing, and empowering families to participate in all aspects of transition planning and implementation.

5. **Program structures:** Ensuring that program development, strategic planning, and evaluation are based on an inclusive, culturally sensitive, and outcome-based philosophy.

Schools that want to expand the effectiveness of their transition practices can find many resources on the web and in the professional literature. When district leaders ask me where they should start or which programs are most likely to result in measurable gains, I refer them to the work of the federally funded National Technical Assistance Center for Transition (NTACT).

NTACT conducts intensive reviews of transition research. Their staff evaluates peer-reviewed, published studies against standards for quality research. They compile summaries of resources on topics such as transition planning, increasing graduation rates, and indicators of post-school success. From the studies that met their standards, they identified 20 predictors for post-school success in employment, further education, and independent living. Based on documented successful practices, new promising transition programs are established by school leaders who partner with families, advocates, and outside organizations. However, many schools still struggle with sustainable funding.

Improving Post-school Outcomes

If we are committed to going beyond compliance with federal regulations to meet the spirit of the law, students need to be included with the end in mind. That means that all faculty and staff will look for ways to reinforce the skills and knowledge students need to develop now for a successful transition into adulthood. Inclusive settings, like the ones they will encounter in adult life, are the perfect place for students to develop these skills. There are three unifying themes that will improve outcomes—relevance, personal development, and self-determination.

Staying Relevant

Teachers who find ways to increase relevance of subject matter for students find that it serves two purposes. First, students become more interested in course content linked to their present or future lives. Across the country, many schools are supporting teachers who use personalized or project-based learning approaches. Many of these approaches engage students in combining new knowledge with problem solving for real-world problems that students might encounter as adults.

Second, grounding students' learning experiences in scenarios where they can solve business or community problems can provide glimpses into future careers. Students tackling those problems can try on possible job assignments to explore whether they would be a good fit. These kinds of experiences often develop into career goals that further increase adolescents' motivation for success in school.

Increasing Personal Development

During secondary school, many students are curious about their own identities that are distinct from their peer group. Teachers who consciously build opportunities for students to develop awareness of themselves as individuals and compassion for individuals who are different from themselves will help prepare them for successful adolescent and adult life.

Galinski (2010) drew on her own expertise with adult skills needed for the 21st century. She spent eight years conducting interviews of more than 70 researchers on children and reviewing more than 1,000 studies about learning. The result was her list of seven essential skills every child needs. I believe these skills, often called executive skills, can be embedded in daily instruction and interactions with both peers and adults. She describes these skills as follows:

1. **Focus and self-control:** Paying attention, remembering the rules, and inhibiting one's initial response to achieve a larger goal.

2. **Perspective taking:** Inhibitory control of your own thoughts and

feelings to consider the perspectives of others, cognitive flexibility to see a situation in different ways, and reflection of someone else's thinking along with your own.

3. **Communicating:** Reflecting upon the goal of what we want to communicate and inhibiting our point of view so that we can understand the viewpoints of others.

4. **Making connections:** Sorting and categorizing information by using working memory to disassemble and recombine elements in new ways.

5. **Critical thinking:** Ongoing search for valid and reliable knowledge to guide beliefs, decisions, and actions.

6. **Taking on challenges:** Developing a mindset that welcomes the stressors of learning and life challenges.

7. **Self-directed, engaged learning:** The ability to use initiative and collaborative skills for lifelong learning.

Brain researchers inform us that these skills are controlled by the prefrontal cortex, which continues to develop well into young adulthood. Those who think that students develop these skills in their early years are missing the opportunity to help youth foster critical abilities. Recent research indicates that development of these executive skills is a better prediction of post-school outcomes than intelligence or academic skills. How could your school promote development of these skills across all subjects and learning activities?

Increasing Self-Determination

There is a growing body of evidence that students with disabilities who develop self-determination skills are more likely to be successful as adults. Wehmeyer, Field, and Thoma (2012) note that self-determination "is volitional, intentional, and self-caused or self-initiated action." Students who exhibit self-determined skills are mindful of their own circumstances, aware of alternatives, able to make choices, and able to advocate for needed supports.

When students with disabilities transition from high school via a diploma, certificate, or by dropping out, they leave the world of service entitlement. They enter the world of service eligibility where they must self-disclose and apply for services. They must submit documentation to prove eligibility for services. This applies to adult disability services that support employment, further education, and independent living.

Years ago, before I knew better, I took my special education responsibilities to mean that I should ensure that my students would not face failure. I provided accommodations and supports that they needed without conferring with them. I assumed responsibility for managing their time, attention, and work effort through my classroom organization structures. I intervened when they had disputes with peers or other adults. In short, my good intentions decreased the chances that my students would develop executive or self-determination skills they would need for adulthood. We learn more from our mistakes than our successes. If well-meaning adults shield them from making choices and directing their own supports, they are unlikely to develop self-management skills.

Students can also be given leadership roles during their IEP meetings with mentoring from a special educator or transition coordinator. These roles provide them with opportunities to take charge of their educational experiences. Self-determination practices must be developed on an ongoing basis with guidance from knowledgeable teachers and family members.

Rather than enabling students to simply fulfill course requirements, teachers can support them to use assignments and test preparation as a context for developing awareness of their own interpersonal and learning approaches. Teachers can encourage them to discover how their disability impacts their ability to learn new vocabulary and curricular concepts. With support, students can become aware of their habitual approaches to long-term projects and make meaningful connections between prior knowledge and new concepts. With guidance, youth can explore the accommodations or learning strategies that work best for them to acquire new knowledge and skills. They can identify which executive skills are strongest and which need to be strengthened.

A FIRST-HAND ACCOUNT OF THE EVOLUTION OF INCLUSION

Experience is the hardest kind of teacher. It gives you the test first and the lesson afterwards.

BRIGHAM YOUNG

Where is that line between those of us who are able and those who are disabled? All human beings have strengths and weaknesses, but those who function successfully find ways to accentuate their strengths and compensate for their weaknesses. We don't include a list of our flaws as part of our self-introductions. We don't approach a job interview announcing our weaknesses.

We build on our strengths to function in life, but it's a different story for those who live with a disability. I remember a gut-wrenching moment in 1984 sitting in my obstetrician's office. The test results were back—I had gestational diabetes. I thought, "Diabetes? A distant aunt had diabetes that led to foot amputation." The doctor was still talking, but I was spinning in a fog. His voice was diminished by the roar of my pounding heart. I cringed with the frightening visions of my life as a cripple. I was thinking, "What happens after losing a foot? How could I care for my baby if I couldn't walk? How could I make a living if I couldn't teach?"

After a seeming lifetime of agony, my doctor's voice sliced through to ask if I was all right. "You just told me that I have diabetes," I said. "How can I be all right?"

"Oh no," he said. "You have gestational diabetes. It's not uncommon with pregnancy. It will go away as soon as you deliver your baby. Your pancreas can't handle the extra weight, that's all. Don't worry."

For that brief moment, I lived in the culture of crippleness. In that place all my dreams and hopes were dashed. My future was shadowed by hopelessness and dependency. All my skills, gifts, and talents disappeared. Historic beliefs about disability enveloped me. I thought I was doomed. I was lucky that my visit there was temporary. Many children with disabilities and their families may live there permanently.

My mentor, Art Nierenberg, invited our leadership training group to examine the invisible cultural beliefs about disability that interfere with striving for and achieving possibilities. We uncovered the pervasive hopelessness embedded in this culture that impacts everyone, including children, families, teachers, medical personnel, and employers. I've learned that when we can name the false negative assumptions embedded in that culture, we have a choice about whether they will limit our aspirations. We can declare them a lie.

No one disputes that the first special education law created educational opportunities for children with disabilities who previously had been excluded from public education. At the same time, the special education system we've created has perpetuated a culture focused on individual weaknesses, "brokenness," and low expectations that has limited our success and negatively impacted the lives of tens of thousands of children and their families. When a doctor or an IEP team stamps a disability label across a child's forehead, there is a danger that we convey the following three unspoken messages to the child and family:

1. You are broken and your weaknesses are greater than your strengths.

2. You need our help and our help will lead to a lifetime of dependency.

3. Your future dreams are unrealistic.

In essence, we invite these children and their families to reduce their expectations. Many families and youth describe a feeling of devastation and hopelessness.

I invite you to take a walk in my shoes. See the world before special education, before inclusion, and during early inclusive experiments. My hope is that we can all learn from past experiences and see a more productive way forward.

Teaching English Before a Special Education Law

When I began teaching junior high school English in 1970, most children that fit within today's category of "invisible" disabilities (i.e., learning disabilities, emotional disturbance, attention deficit hyperactivity disorder, and autism spectrum) were not considered disabled. In Figure 2.1, you can see how students were considered within the range of normal and taught with everyone else unless the school offered a slow or basic class.

Figure 2.1

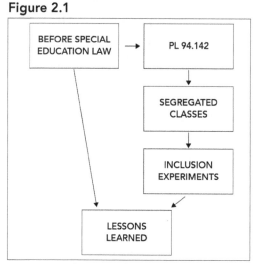

My first year I taught English wearing miniskirts, spiked heels, and a ponytail. I was 22, waspy, athletic, and barely taller than my 7th-grade students. I taught five classes in a seven-period day, including one 9th-grade gifted class, one 7th-grade basic class, and three 7th-grade average classes. I also had one duty period. Those classes amounted to three preparations each day. Today, many teachers' unions have negotiated for a maximum of two preparations, but back then, I felt lucky that I didn't have five different preps like some of my colleagues.

I spent my one planning period learning the English curriculum for both 7th and 9th grade, locating materials that hadn't been returned to the book room, planning lessons and tests, and keeping up with grading. It was overwhelming, all consuming, and I loved every minute. I was playing school in real life.

My favorite class by far was my basic class. Their writing samples were tangles of incomplete phrases and run-on sentences. I made cartoon posters of the six basic sentence types, and they practiced expanding them with creative adjectives and adverbs. Sometimes we got silly inserting strings of prepositional phrases.

When I broke complex ideas into step-by-step directions, I discovered that my basic class flourished. Some other teachers saw them as behavior problems, but I noticed they only acted out when confronted with certain failure. I built relationships with my students based on mutual respect. I believed they all could learn, and I structured activities to help them build mastery. Success was attainable in my room, and their eagerness to learn inspired my creativity.

In those days, I had a curriculum guide developed by summer teacher teams that listed the concepts and skills I was expected to teach, but there were no curriculum pacing manuals and no state tests. There was large variation in the skills individual students brought to my class, but none of them had labels. Teachers were trusted to do their best to teach all their students, and we trusted our students to do whatever they needed to do to learn.

Understanding the First Special Education Law

By the 1970s, there were just a few schools or separate classrooms for children with visible disabilities (e.g., children who were blind or deaf, had cerebral palsy, or were labeled as retarded, which was a word used regularly at the time). Most of these schools had been funded by parents or schools pressured by family groups.

Art Nierenberg had helped establish the groundbreaking Viscardi Center in New York City for children with disabilities in the 1960s. When it first opened, he was shocked to discover that some of his adolescent students were brought to school wearing pajamas. According to their parents, these children had never been outside their homes and previously had no need for street clothes or shoes. By the 1970s, many parents across the country accepted that their children were too disabled to be educated and kept them home.

All this changed in my third year of teaching. The district special education supervisor announced to our faculty the enactment of a new law—*The Education of the Handicapped Act of 1975* (P.L. 94-142). He told us that children with disabilities who had previously been kept home would now be attending school. My colleagues and I exchanged nervous glances with raised eyebrows. He described new invisible disabilities recognized under this law such as learning disabilities and other health impairments, including attention deficit hyperactivity disorder.

I was intrigued about this new law, and the kids like Dale, the endearing boy in the second row of my third-period English class, who struggled with weak literacy skills. I decided to pursue a second graduate degree in special education focused on reading and learning disabilities. I pictured myself, armed with these new skills, becoming one of those heroic teachers who could salvage struggling children.

In my seventh year, with my graduate coursework preparation behind me and now certified in special education, I launched a pilot regional program for 14 junior high students. These students had been officially diagnosed with learning disabilities, attention deficit hyperactivity disorder, and behavioral disorders. Based on recommendations from Individualized Education Program (IEP) teams, my students were eligible to receive special education services for the first time in their lives.

I was responsible for teaching my students English, math, social studies, science, and study skills using curriculum guides for 7th, 8th, and 9th grades. Basically, my students and I faced each other five periods a day. Since the law required individualized instruction for each student's grade level, I created massive organizational systems. I could not have survived without Rose, my paraprofessional and sidekick. She would ask what I had in mind and then jump in wholeheartedly. In tandem, we managed behavior, provided individual tutoring, monitored practice, graded student work, and tracked progress.

Since I was only certified to teach English, planning for math, social studies, and science was a challenge. Luckily, Doug, the science teacher across the hall, saved my life. We traded rooms on Thursdays so my students could do experiments he designed in his lab. In return, I developed detailed, step-by-step instructions that Doug used with all his classes.

The huge differences in my students' math proficiency made simultaneously teaching three grades of math harder. Using results from a diagnostic math test, Rose and I created sets of worksheets with illustrated explanations of math processes at the top and calculations and word problems to solve at the bottom. At the beginning of each math period, each student picked up his math folder and got started. We spent that class circulating as individual tutors with boxes of manipulative shapes. Each afternoon, we checked their work and put their next day's worksheet in the folder.

These were students who reached junior high having lived with failure and humiliation for years. These students were newly eligible for special education service, and they arrived in my room convinced that they were stupid and incapable. Some were passive aggressive and others simply felt hopeless. They were angry and defiant when I pressed them to work on skills they thought were sure failure for them. But I could be as stubborn as they were, and I wouldn't give up on them.

We set up a reward system with points for completing work and demonstrating appropriate classroom behavior. We agreed on expectations and positive rewards. I still remember the system. The students could cash in 15 points for a pen or pencil and 30 points for fun activities such as playing educational games instead of worksheets. Some students cashed in points as soon as they were accumulated, but other students delayed gratification for the ultimate prize worth 300 points. I would drive to their home on a Friday night, meet their families and pets, admire their trophies and hobbies, and take them to one of the newly opened fast food restaurants for dinner of their choice.

The word spread, so half my class would also show up and sit in neighboring booths. My students would gleefully blow cigarette smoke at us (smoking was not prohibited in public buildings in the 1970s). These teenagers became more than students to me. During the three years that we were together, they made remarkable growth in their skills and greater strides in their self-worth. In the process, they taught me so much about teaching.

What I want you to take away from this story is the joyous experience of being clear about my mission. I was given the responsibility and freedom to create a system—a safety net for my students. I was determined to fix my students' weaknesses so they could return to the general education classroom and be successful. My students desperately wanted to become "normal" and were relieved that working with me would get them get there. They wanted to escape the culture of crippleness.

My principal and district special education supervisor recognized that nobody had taken on this teaching assignment before, and they entrusted me to figure it out. The challenge drew on my creativity and stretched my capacity to develop structures and routines that my students needed even more than those I previously taught in my English classroom. I was determined to not let anybody down, most importantly, my students. I can't describe the satisfaction of being trusted and striving to prove myself in a way that made a difference for my students. It didn't occur to me to question whether my students could be fixed. I hadn't met Art Nierenberg yet. I didn't know that we were up against the culture of crippleness. I believed in my mission wholeheartedly.

Understanding Separate is Not Equal

Originally, special education was equated with a separate classroom, wing, or school. Those first special education classrooms were a haven for students with disabilities who had been called lazy, stupid, slow, or problem children before being assigned a disability label. In those protected settings, students experienced relief from the embarrassment of learning problems.

The district where I worked created dedicated classrooms to address the needs of students who required special education supports to be successful. Many districts even built separate schools for students who had more complex needs with staff trained to work with that particular population. Most of the staff that worked in those settings were well trained, highly competent, and deeply committed.

Several issues became apparent with this separate special education classroom system. Teachers and school leaders poured their passionate problem-solving skills into their work and believed there was a solution just out of reach. But students weren't leaving special education classrooms equipped with skills to succeed. Most students who were labeled as disabled remained in special education classrooms for the rest of their schooling. Many students dropped out because they were frustrated with a system that didn't fit them. Those students who did graduate had limited success in adult settings.

Disability advocates cited *Brown v. Board of Education* and began to protest that students educated in separate special education classrooms were denied the same education as their non-disabled peers. That 1954 landmark Supreme Court decision had declared that racially separate education for children was not equal. Families and advocates protested that instruction in separate special education classrooms was less rigorous than in general education settings. More importantly, they wanted to reverse the stigma of a disability label. We soon learned that moving students into inclusive settings remedied the separate part, but the stigma persisted, embedded in the invisible culture of crippleness.

With the reauthorization and renaming of the *Individuals with Disabilities Education Act* in 1997 and again in 2004, there were more regulations to encourage including students with disabilities in general education classrooms beside their non-disabled peers. Leaders in the Least Restrictive Environment and Regular Education Initiative movements insisted that special education services be provided within the regular classroom as much as possible. Their slogan was "Special education is a service—not a place."

When Mingling Is Insufficient

While working as a transition coordinator, I followed inclusive experiments in local schools and saw that students who had been effectively included were more successful when I placed them in job sites. They knew how to ask fellow workers for help and were more likely to exhibit appropriate social skills for the job.

Salend and Duhaney (1999) conducted a literature review of studies on the impact of inclusion on students with and without disabilities and their educators. They defined inclusion as "a movement that seeks to create schools and other social institutions based on meeting the needs of all learners as well as respecting and learning from each other's differences."

They reported that studies related to academic achievement were mixed. Some students achieved as well as their nondisabled peers while others lagged behind. Likewise, social interaction and peer acceptance were positive in some studies and lacking in others. Sadly, in all studies, students with disabilities reported personal negative experiences, such as peer ridicule and stigmatized status caused by failure or humiliation from reduced expectations in the general education classroom. Overall, researchers cited the difficulty of evaluating the accuracy of studies because of high variability in service delivery models. There was no standard model for inclusive services.

According to this same literature review, Salend and Duhaney (1999) reported that inclusive instruction had no adverse effect on the academic achievement of students without disabilities. Survey results of these students indicated their positive views of inclusion, stating "increased acceptance, understanding, and tolerance of individual differences..."

Finally, Salend and Duhaney (1999) reviewed studies that investigated special and general educators' perceptions of inclusion. Again, variability was found. They state, "Teachers' perceptions of inclusion seem to be related to their success in implementing inclusion, to student characteristics, and to the availability of financial resources, instructional and ancillary supportive services, training, administrative support, and time to collaborate and communicate with others."

Since 2000, I have taught university courses focused on skills and strategies useful for inclusive settings. I have supervised over 100 graduate interns teaching in inclusive classrooms. I have provided consultative coaching to teachers and school leaders in several states. Based on my experiences, I am sad to say that the perceptions and issues reported in those studies are just as true today as they were decades ago. The effectiveness of inclusion as measured by students' achievement and teachers' perception of their own success is highly variable.

Simply intermingling students with disabilities into the general education classroom is insufficient. Teachers need to become proficient with methods for managing classroom dynamics and instructional strategies that reach all learners. If they are expected to collaborate both inside and outside the classroom, these students need support in becoming proficient with those unfamiliar interpersonal skills. School leaders' role in establishing the vision, ground rules, and climate for nurturing creative problem solving in their buildings can't be underestimated.

Lessons Learned

We have learned so much in the more than 40 years since the first special education law, but what we've learned hasn't translated into our results. Why? As I reflect on my years of experience in a variety of roles, I believe the answer has three parts, as depicted in Figure 2.2. First, we need to rethink our construct of disability. Second, we need to use a unified, non-fragmented approach to instruction with special education as an integral, unified component. Third, we need to clarify the intent of special education services. If we want to improve the effectiveness of our work and improve post-school outcomes for students with disabilities, we need to reconsider some basic assumptions that undermine our work with students.

Figure 2.2

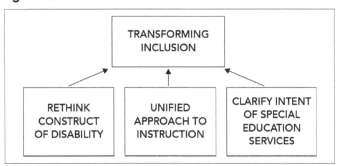

Rethinking Our Construct of Disability

Repair shop thinking is common in our society. When our car, refrigerator, or computer malfunctions, we turn to experts who diagnose and fix the problem. When we feel sick, we seek a doctor to diagnose and cure our ailments. After listing our symptoms, we undergo tests to investigate the source of our complaints. Then we expect doctors to give us a diagnosis. Further, we will go to great lengths to find a medical practitioner who can treat and cure our condition.

Similarly, the belief that students with disabilities are broken and need to be fixed is pervasive within disability systems. Special education identification procedures require schools to assess and identify specific symptoms, match them with criteria for disability labels, and decide whether the condition warrants special education services. I remember many instances of participating in team debates about whether a student's weakness was severe enough to qualify. If not, they were left on their own to sink or swim in the general education classroom. Luckily, this phenomenon has changed recently with Response to Intervention (RTI) systems in many places.

However, if the student is found eligible, the team develops an IEP focused on how special education and related services will remediate or foster improvement of those identified skill sets. If we recognize any strengths in the student, they are listed, but viewed as irrelevant to our discussion at the special education team meeting.

Parents frequently hoped and expected that we would fix their child's disability. As years progressed, they were disappointed to learn that the condition might be permanent. I can recall discussions around high school IEP tables when parents were outright angry that we hadn't fixed their child's problems yet. They, too, wanted to escape the culture of crippleness.

It is time to confront the culture of crippleness head-on. We need to acknowledge that disability labels may be required to secure special education funding, but they do not predict the future. By working in partnership, we can empower all youth, including those with disabilities, to reject the shame of a disability label and define who they are as unique human beings with futures full of possibilities and adequacy. We have to see what we are up against to choose a different, more hopeful path.

Aronson's (2002) theory of Stereotype Threat is relevant here. Stereotypes are those generalized ideas we all have about groups of people that rarely hold true when applied to an individual. For example, grandmothers have white hair, wear aprons, and bake cookies. But there are other unconsciously held stereotypes that influence how we view people and their possibilities, such as boys have trouble sitting still, girls are not as good in science, and Asian students are conscientious scholars. In Aronson's words, "Negative stereotypes alleging low intelligence among blacks and Latinos are particularly problematic, both because intelligence is universally validated and because these stereotypes are so widely known." Many studies have provided evidence that stereotyped prejudices influence teachers' relationships and expectations for students, even if they don't believe the stereotype.

Aronson investigated the influence of stereotypes on the person's own performance. He defines Stereotype Threat as "apprehensiveness about confirming a stereotype, both in my own eyes and other people's eyes." While his research focused on stereotypes related to gender, race, and ethnicity, I believe his findings relate to the culture of crippleness. For example, he reports that students who experience Stereotype Threat are "hyperaware of people's negative expectations for their group....Given this climate of stereotype awareness, there are ample grounds for black and Latino students to feel a burden of suspicion, to feel at risk of confirming stereotypes through their behavior, and to wonder if they belong in environments where academic ability is prized." Could the same be said of students with disabilities?

He describes studies of test taking in which college students who experienced Stereotype Threat performed lower than expected, although they described trying harder because of the burden to disprove the stereotype. Through interviews, researchers learned that in addition to their thinking related to the test, these students deal with anxiety that their poor performance could confirm the stereotype. But Stereotype Threat can be experienced by anyone. In the following study, Aronson (2002) describes a study of white males:

> In a simple experiment, I performed with my colleagues...we asked highly competent white males, (both at Stanford University and the University of Texas) to take a difficult math test. Two groups were told that the test was aimed at determining their math abilities. For one group we added a Stereotype Threat: we told them that one of our reasons for doing the research was to understand why Asians seemed to perform better on these tests. In this condition, these test-takers stumbled on the test. Pressured by the stereotype of Asian mathematical superiority, they solved significantly fewer of the problems on the test and felt less confident about their performance. These students were highly competent and confident males; most of them were mathematics majors and most of them had earned near-perfect scores on the math portion of the SAT.

Over time, Aronson reports, vulnerable students may develop the following four self-defeating defenses to avoid experiencing stereotype threat:

1. **Self-handicapping:** Making claims that some external factor impeded their performance (e.g., "The sun was in my eyes." "The test was biased." or "I didn't study enough.")

2. **Avoidance of challenge:** Arranging things to have the least risk of confirming the stereotype (e.g., I'll choose the easier project so I won't risk a poor grade or looking stupid.)

3. **Self-suppression:** Coping by suppressing, adjusting, or concealing themselves to better fit the image of those who belong (e.g., I just don't talk in class to avoid the looks when I give a wrong answer.)

4. **Disidentification:** Devaluing an achievement to protect one's self-esteem (e.g., I don't care if I can't do math. It's not important for my life.)

All these defenses protect students from the shame of Stereotype Threat, but they also pose a barrier to academic and social success in school. Aronson (2002) offers teachers the following ways to reduce stereotype threat:

- **Reduce diagnosticity:** Relieving students' anxiety of diagnosis by stating that high stakes tests are to measure teachers' effectiveness, not students' abilities. Avoid mentioning that tests will be used to compare subgroups of students.

- **Use learning curve protection:** Assuring students that they are making gains in their mastery.

- **Teach malleable skills versus fixed ability:** Asserting that the skill being measured is malleable (i.e., growth mindset) and that students' efforts will increase their competence over time.

- **Build peer group support:** Creating a peer group of students who face a common Stereotype Threat, in which they receive messages of belonging, share about common problems, and participate in instruction of advanced material to confirm teachers' high expectations.

- **Promote cooperation rather than competition:** Getting students to work cooperatively on challenging learning to increase achievement and a sense of belonging.

Developing a Unified Approach

Research has provided a rich supply of strategies and approaches that have been shown to be effective in instruction and classroom management of all youth, especially those with disabilities. However, I believe that school leaders and their faculty are overwhelmed with the deluge of good ideas they should implement in their classrooms. To illustrate, I did a quick internet search for federally funded education resource centers and found the following resources:

- **The What Works Clearinghouse of the Institute of Educational Sciences (IES)** reviews educational research and provides information on proven programs, products, practices, and policies in education.
- **The National Technical Assistance Center for Transition** posts evidence-based practices contributing to positive post-school outcomes.
- **The Regional Comprehensive Centers** provides frontline assistance to build states' capacity to support school improvement.
- **The Content Centers** support states with building state capacity and productivity; college and career readiness and success; enhancing early learning outcomes, great teachers and leaders, innovations in learning and school turnaround; and improving standards and assessments implementation.

In addition, there are federally funded centers focusing on parent information and training, equity, homeless education, positive behavior supports, bullying prevention, and postsecondary education for individuals with disabilities.

The purpose of this book is to integrate all these separate bodies of wisdom. Teachers and school leaders can begin viewing school improvement as a unified system intent on empowering youth to develop skills they will need throughout their education and into adult environments. The education of students with disabilities must be viewed as the responsibility of the whole school community, including all faculty members, school leaders, families, and community resources.

The Special Education Mission

Many special educators I have worked with over the years are confused about their job. Early in my special education career, I thought my job was to remediate the weaknesses of students with disabilities, catch them up, and return them to general education classrooms. My passion to achieve that goal motivated me to develop creative classroom structures to meet my students' needs. Ultimately, I failed. My students were not repaired. They were not able to become "normal" and perform like all the other students.

Special education law calls special educators to be responsible for "specially designed instruction," which is defined as "adapting, as appropriate, to the needs of an eligible child...the content, methodology, or delivery of instruction (i) to address the unique needs of the child that result from the child's disability; and (ii) to ensure access of the child to the general curriculum, so that the child can meet the educational standard ...that apply to all children." (IDEA, 2004).

Special educators are not charged with repairing students' disabilities. Professionals must ensure that they identify each student's unique needs and gifts. Special educators must become increasingly proficient in methods for adapting content and methods of instruction so that those students can achieve rigorous standards. In order to accomplish this mission, they will need ongoing support for continuous professional development and reflective practice.

The bottom line is that special educators, in concert with other professionals and families, will support youths to navigate out of the culture of crippleness. They will coach them to identify their unique gifts, develop strategies to compensate for their disabling conditions, and foster a network of peer and adult supports. I believe this approach will provide special educators a rewarding career and combat prevailing burnout.

School leaders who want to expand teachers' capacity will create a professional learning climate infused with trust and safety to experiment. I will provide structures that support the change process in upcoming chapters.

When I began teaching English in the early 1970s, teachers were responsible for designing instruction to meet the needs of all students who showed up. These classes had wide diversity, but no disability labels. Those of us who were successful with struggling students used organizing structures to break down complex ideas. We encouraged peer support and developed relationships with our students as individuals. We held high expectations based on the belief that with professional support and focused work ethic, all students could succeed. The trust and humanity in my school was rewarding and nurtured my creativity.

The first special education law required states to provide education for all students with disabilities, but it also perpetuated the cultural perception that students with a disability label are broken and special educators will fix them. Research on inclusive practices revealed inconsistent results for youth with disabilities and mixed perceptions of teachers.

Schools that want to create more effective inclusive programs for students with disabilities will address the following three issues—rethinking our construct of disability, unifying school improvement activities, and clarifying the mission of special education.

CHAPTER THREE

SYSTEMS THINKING FOR INCLUSION

The whole is greater than the sum of its parts.

ARISTOTLE

Was it a coincidence that I met my husband as I was learning about using a systems approach to inclusion? Robert is a consulting systems engineer who helps companies problem solve issues in their manufacturing or refining of metals. His skills are highly specialized, and there is very little new blood coming into his field. He tells people he's like the last watchmaker. But unlike most of the educators I know, he creates mental pictures of how systems intersect. When we first met, he started asking me questions about how all the pieces of education, especially special education, fit together. His questions stretched my thinking as I refined my big picture of inclusion.

Social scientists use the term "fundamental attribution error" to describe solutions that blame one group of stakeholders (i.e., it's the teachers' fault or the parents') or a single factor (i.e., poverty, lack of technology, or literacy curriculum) for a complex social problem. In fact, if we aim to improve the outcomes for youth, including those with disabilities, we must use a systems approach to consider the problems we face, the strategies we need to change, and the humane mechanisms we will use to support individuals at the center – the teachers, leaders, families, and students.

It's important to view inclusion as a system. All the parts work together, like the human body. If you seek a fitness coach, he would advise you about exercise, diet, and a lifestyle balance of a challenging vocation with social activities, relaxation, and sufficient sleep. Attending to only one aspect of the whole picture may solve one problem in the short term, but you need to incorporate all components if you want a healthy lifestyle. In the same way, if the school improvement plan only focuses on one component, it would be difficult to build and sustain an inclusive system. Figure 3.1 shows an overview of an inclusive system.

Figure 3.1

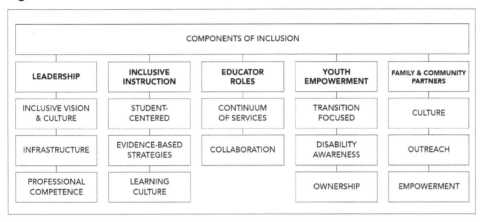

Beginning with Leadership

There is no point in going any further if the principal and leadership team are not taking the lead. Teachers take their cue from the principal. What he reinforces during faculty meetings and Monday memos will alert faculty to what he considers important. The principal is the building's leader in vision, school culture, infrastructure, and professional competence.

Creating an Inclusive Vision and Culture

The principal's vision of an inclusive school will set the tone for the building. What does your school vision statement say? What routine practices bring it to life? Is it clear to the faculty, lunch ladies, bus drivers, and families that all students belong in this school? If your school includes a minority population, what steps are taken to ensure that these students and their families feel welcome? Are your staff members using terms that marginalize students? Are there clues in your bulletin boards and newsletters that identify students as "different"? Are students called "the special ed kids" or some other term that separates them? Has your principal taken a leadership role in bringing your school vision into reality so that all students experience belonging?

The school's vision is the foundation for a pervasive culture across the building. I have been in schools where the teachers and students were clearly partners in learning. The children in these environments felt safe to make mistakes and learn from them. I have been in other schools where the levels of frustration and antagonism were uncomfortable. How would you describe your building culture? Are there practices in place that prepare your students to become tolerant citizens of a changing world?

Maslow's hierarchy of needs ranks safety as the second level after basic survival needs are met. The safety level includes "security of body, employment, resources, morality, family, health, and property." Do all students, especially those students with disabilities, feel safe in your classrooms? Many schools have instituted anti-bullying programs as an extension of their vision that all students belong. There are wonderful resources on the web to start such a program in your building. Preventing bullying is a good place to start, but establishing a culture of belonging and safety will take collective efforts of faculty, families, and community members.

Building an Infrastructure

Inclusion can't flourish in a vacuum. Schools with strong infrastructures set conditions for teachers to implement inclusive practices and for all students to learn. Three important aspects of infrastructure for inclusion are the master schedule, professional development, and professional collaboration.

School leaders have options for organizing their master schedules. Elementary and middle schools are more likely to consider the needs of special populations first. After considering students' support needs, they plan how to allocate their special educators, and then they construct the master schedule. Prioritizing special needs students is harder for high schools dedicated to vocational courses, international baccalaureate, or performing arts. If there is only one section of cosmetology, marching band, or Chinese II, those classes will be scheduled first. Whatever system for scheduling is used, if students with disabilities are an afterthought, the infrastructure most likely will not support inclusive practice.

Principals often ask my advice about how to schedule their special educators. I recommend that schools begin with a collaborative activity, creating a list of their students with special needs grouped by their accommodations, academic, technological, and behavioral needs. Once teachers and administrators know how many students will need coteaching support or monitoring for a specific subject, they can make decisions about teacher allocation.

Developing Professional Competence

What the principal looks for during formal observations and pre- and post observation conferences will be shared through the building underground communication. Topics selected for professional development should align with building priorities and improvement plans. Today, there are many expectations placed on schools. More than ever, teachers need a thoughtful principal to bring clear focus for their school's direction.

Three years ago, I gave nearly identical workshops on learning stations in two schools. In School A, teachers arrived already talking about how they would implement new approaches. The principal stayed for the whole workshop and brainstormed with her teachers. At the end, she asked to be invited when they experimented with stations in their classrooms. In contrast, I never saw the principal at School B. Teachers asked me how long they had to stay. When I compared the exit ticket responses for the same workshop, teachers in School A raved about my workshop and wrote extended notes about their plans for implementation while School B's responses were curt and critical. Since that experience, I'm very reluctant to conduct a workshop unless the principal or another leader has endorsed the topic and prepared the teachers to fully engage in learning with me.

As teachers assemble before my workshops, I often ask them how many initiatives their building has this year. I'm not surprised anymore when they start counting them off and run out of fingers. If the principal and leadership team haven't established clear expectations for professional growth, teachers become selective about how they will use their precious time.

The problem is that professional development is not one size fits all. Some teachers are early adopters of creative approaches and others prefer to stay in their comfort zones. Special educators gain recognition for their expertise when given leadership roles with strategies for diverse learners. I've seen the best results with schools that embed practices into structured professional learning communities where experienced teachers mentor teachers who are just beginning to experiment with new strategies. ESSA 2015 encourages states and districts to establish practices that provide administrative support for implementation, such as opportunities for peer feedback to improve collaborative lesson plans and videotaped lessons.

Adopting Inclusive Instruction

Many students with disabilities perform better in classrooms that employ a student-centered approach, evidence-based practices, and learning culture.

Using a Student-Centered Approach

Teachers make choices daily about strategies for introducing new knowledge and skills, opportunities to practice learning and deepen understanding, and methods to evaluate progress. Unfortunately, most teachers use teacher-centered approaches because that's how they were taught and they think it gives them the most control over what happens in their classroom.

As teachers learn about and begin experimenting with student-centered approaches, they report that it shifts their effectiveness and satisfaction with teaching. Teacher-centered instruction focuses on the knowledge and skills teachers have to pass on to students. The sage-on-the stage approach demonstrates, explains, gives examples, and links new information with prior knowledge. In student-centered learning, teachers prompt youth to explore ideas, make meaning of new information, and form their own connections. Student-centered approaches are based on teachers' awareness of the diversity of each student's abilities, prior knowledge, and learning preferences. Teachers become more than the "guide-on-the-side" in student-centered classrooms, they become instructional codesigners in partnership with the learners.

Employing Evidence-based Practices

The last two decades have produced a wealth of information about instructional practices that work. Recent legislation requires teachers to base their curricular objectives on rigorous standards and 21st-century outcomes. Teachers benefit from guidance on planning their instructional methodology. The McREL What Works Clearinghouse has summarized findings of educational research into recommendations for instructional strategies.

The national centers for Universal Design for Learning (UDL) and Response to Intervention (RtI) offer resources for scaffolding complex instruction that address individual student needs and spark student engagement. The Center for Applied Special Technology (CAST) describes UDL as "a framework to improve and optimize teaching and learning for all people based on scientific insights into how humans learn." It has replaced differentiation as an approach for addressing differences in students' readiness, interests, and learning preferences. The concept, taken from architecture, is that a building equipped with a ramp accommodates a mother pushing her stroller, a deliveryman dropping off heavy packages, and someone who uses a wheelchair. Teachers who use UDL, plan for universal access to engagement, representation, action, and expression in their learning.

The RTI Network describes Response to Intervention (RtI) as a "multitier approach to early identification and support of students with learning and behavior needs." Schools that establish such practices use data to screen all students, provide appropriate interventions, and monitor progress.

Another term adopted from architecture and construction is scaffolding. When workers are building or repairing a tall building, they construct a scaffolded walkway first. They stand on this structure to get their job done. When they are finished, they remove the scaffolding and the building stands independently. In the same way, many learners use scaffolding to learn complex skills and knowledge.

Teachers are delighted when scaffolded structures help all students achieve. Examples include comparison-contrast graphic organizers for planning composition, checklists for a science lab, and a learning map depicting a visual picture of key ideas. At first, teachers provide scaffolding for their students, but then they gradually fade that support and teach students to create their own support structures. I recently heard of a 3rd-grade teacher who introduces an assignment and asks her students to look through their folder of organizers to select the one that matches the day's task. Now that's giving students self-determination skills that they will carry for the rest of their life. Chapter 7 provides more information about these research-based frameworks and approaches. Teachers who integrate structures into their lesson plans will more effectively meet the diverse learning needs of their students.

Establishing a Classroom Learning Culture

The third aspect of effective instruction is establishing a learning culture in the classroom that fosters peer-to-peer support, cooperative learning, and an environment where it is safe to ask for help. As classrooms become more diverse, teachers increasingly use proactive approaches to establishing a climate of welcoming and accommodating differences. Youth are influenced by attitudes of adults as they learn to accept diversity in the classroom.

Research findings indicate that we all learn more in peer cooperative and collaborative groups than from an expert speaker. Chapter 8 describes key principles for managing interpersonal dynamics. I share some exciting procedures that teachers can use to support students to foster strong interactive teaming skills while deepening their mastery of content. These approaches are perfect for teachers who abandoned using ineffective group assignments.

Defining Educators' Roles

Principals and district leaders often ask for my advice about the roles of teachers and others who provide support to special needs students. As schools move forward with inclusion, the roles of all these professionals will change. Once teachers and specialists have sorted students by their support needs, it's time to consider how teachers should be assigned.

Exploring the Continuum of Services

Special education regulations specify that a continuum of placements should be available to serve students with disabilities. Recent thinking translates this from a continuum of settings into a continuum of service intensities. The law encourages IEP teams to provide those services in the general education setting whenever possible to minimize time that students are excluded from the advantages of the regular classroom.

There are different terms to describe the levels of service within the continuum that are offered in comprehensive public schools. I prefer the following terms listed from least to most intensive services:

- **Indirect services:** The general educator receives minimal support for students whose disabilities do not impact achievement in this subject.

For example, if a student has a math disability, she could succeed in most content classes as long as the general educators know how to support her with mathematically based practices.

- **Learning support coach (LSC):** A special educator is assigned to a group of students (sometimes called a caseload) either organized by grade level, content area, or small learning community. The students have dedicated times each week to meet with the special educator individually or in a small coaching group to develop personal executive skills and self-determination. They learn to create their own scaffolds and seek needed supports from peers and their content teacher(s). The special educator also provides coaching to the general educator on scaffolding and UDL, especially related to students on their caseload. As appropriate, the LSC spends time in classes to monitor student progress, reinforce instruction, and support all students.

- **Coteaching:** A special and general educator are scheduled to coteach classes for the students who need increased scaffolding and UDL on an ongoing basis. Both teachers share planning, instruction, assessment, and grading. Both are responsible for drafting IEP goals and monitoring progress. Chapter 6 describes the typical structures that coteachers use for instruction. Note that coteachers *must* have coplanning time at least weekly. Expecting them to coplan on their own time or after school doesn't work in the long run.

- **Resource:** A few special education students need intensive instruction in a separate classroom, taught by a special educator apart from non-disabled peers. As inclusive practices expand, schools have reduced the number of students and reduced the amount of time students spend with resource services.

Expanding Professional Collaboration

As a consultant, one concern I hear repeatedly is about the worth of special educators. How are special educators viewed in your building? Some complain that they don't want to be viewed as assistant teachers by the general educator or by the students. However, they are uncertain of their role. They feel like a visitor or an intruder in someone else's classroom. They worry that their general educator partners will view their suggestions as critical of their teaching competence. They wonder if they should speak up or wait for an invitation to give feedback. General educators complain that they don't want to have someone hovering in the perimeter of their room, interrupting instruction, and criticizing their teaching. Many general education teachers believe it's not their job to tell another certified teacher what to do, so they wait for the special educator to speak up.

In my workshops, I talk about three stages of collaboration (Gately, 2005). In the beginning stage, the two partners are uncomfortable, uncertain, and careful about not offending the other. I prompt them to create ways they can divide routine classroom duties. With the ice broken, teachers design all sorts of creative ways to colead instruction. This is a great beginning.

Special education supports are also provided by paraprofessionals, guidance counselors, nurses, psychologists, behavior specialists, and speech-language, physical, and occupational therapists. As schools make progress with inclusion, more of those services are provided in the general education settings. I provide more strategies for expanding collaboration in Chapter 5.

Youth Empowerment

If we are committed to improving post-school outcome statistics for youth with disabilities and increasing the degree to which they are integrated into adult settings, we have to start with what happens in school.

Focusing on Transition

In many cases youth and their families are not prepared for the loss of supports that occurs when students leave high school. From birth, students with disabilities who are determined eligible for special education services are entitled to free appropriate public education (FAPE). Each state publishes IDEA procedural safeguards with federal and state guidelines for identification, individual educational programs, annual reviews, and dispute resolution. Parents' complaints about noncompliant actions can become expensive, therefore it's important for schools and districts to take steps to ensure that students' and families' rights are protected.

Students with disabilities exit from public school in three ways—with a diploma, a certificate stating that they have reached maximum public education age, or as a dropout. Once they have exited, they are no longer eligible for the protections of IDEA. They move from the world of entitlement to the world of eligibility. Agencies that provide adult service supports related to employment, further education, and independent living (e.g., residential, transportation, medical, and recreation) are only an option if the individual applies and meets the eligibility criteria for that particular agency.

Too often students and their families have become accustomed to following the school's lead in the provision of special education services. In the adult world of services, no one will seek them out and offer services. For some services, they must apply to get on the waiting list for years before they graduate. For other services the youth must self disclose and provide documentation to prove they are eligible. While special education services in the prekindergarten to high school world are free for all who qualify, adult services may be limited by available funds and may require a copayment. Agencies may also have policies to serve only those within a particular demographic or specific diagnoses.

As a college professor, I could not ask any of my students if they had disabilities, no matter what I suspected. To do so would be a violation of their privacy. This would be the same as asking their religion, ethnicity, or sexual orientation. If a student needed an accommodation, such as a copy of my lecture notes or extended time on an exam, he or she must self-advocate. Students would need to go to the Office of Disabilities Services (ODS) on campus. There are different names at different colleges, but every college that receives any federal funds must have such an office.

If there was sufficient evidence that the student needed accommodations, the ODS counselor would prepare a letter stating the needed accommodations. If students gave me the letter and I refused to provide those accommodations, I could be personally sued under the *Americans with Disabilities Act*. If students did not self-disclose for whatever reason, I would have no obligation to provide them any accommodations. Do your college-bound students know to take documentation of their disability (e.g., medical, psychological, or mental health evaluations) to ODS?

Increasing Disability Awareness

When I was a special education teacher, despite my best intentions, I unknowingly let my students down. I was diligent about discerning the needs of each one of them and providing individualized services and accommodations. I knew that James needed to maintain eye contact with me during directions or he wouldn't know where to start. I knew that Charlene needed a seat away from the noisy distraction of the pencil sharpener. I knew that Stefan needed frequent opportunities to summarize our reading in his own words. I knew Quantell needed wait time before she responded to questions. I managed all those different learning needs, but we never discussed them. I never told them what I was doing for each of them, nor did I ever ask if my strategies worked for them.

Then I became a transition coordinator and listened to complaints from disability service providers in higher education and vocational rehabilitation. I realized what a disservice I had done to all those students. I started encouraging secondary teachers, guidance counselors, and families to talk with their teenagers—the earlier the better—about their specific disability. These young people need to know the terms used in their diagnosis and the ways that their disability impacts their learning and functioning. Most importantly, they need to know how to use their strengths to their advantage.

Encouraging Students to Take Ownership

How are students prepared to self-disclose and self-advocate in your school? All students can practice ownership of their own learning if teachers involve them in formative assessments, especially if they learn to seek and use feedback. For students with disabilities, self-determination and ownership skills start with understanding and acceptance of the implications of their own disabilities. In addition, students need awareness of the culture of crippleness and the associated stigma that they may encounter across their whole lives. Finally, students need opportunities to make choices and the wisdom of coaches who can mentor them as they practice assuming ownership for their own learning and success.

Recent brain research has provided so much exciting information about the learning process. When we foster our students' knowledge of their own learning process, called metacognition, they become empowered and less passive about their education. They can become advocates for the scaffolding and accommodations they need. In many places today, students practice their advocacy skills by leading all or part of their IEP meetings.

Family and Community Partners

As a parent of two young adults who were diagnosed with disabilities during their school years, I have a personal appreciation for how families are treated. I had already been a special educator for 12 years when I attended my first IEP meeting as a parent.

Sitting in the parent seat was a vulnerable, eye-opening experience. I saw professionals who interacted with certainty when I knew they couldn't guarantee that proposed methods would accomplish the stated goals. I longed to tell my story so that they would understand what brought us to this point, but the meeting was too impersonal. As they recited what my son couldn't do, I felt exposed and blamed for my parenting deficits. Unspoken negative communication rang loudly in my ears and was compounded by my awareness that as a professional I had treated parents the same way.

A 2006 publication summarizing investigative research into effective ways to address student achievement gaps proposed that policy maker look to family engagement efforts. They said,

> "This report is a call to action. It entreats people at the federal, state and local levels to seize the moment, to mobilize on behalf of children - especially those who are disadvantaged - and to make parent power a central theme in the effort to improve academic performance" (Coleman et al, 2006).

These conclusions equally apply to creating successful, inclusive programs and improving postsecondary outcomes for youth with disabilities.

Building a Supportive Culture

A critical aspect of building an inclusive culture in a school is ensuring that families and community organizations are included as partners. I've coauthored and coedited several publications about engaging families as partners during the secondary transition years. They all start with building a relationship with families based on awareness that past relationships may have been disempowering. Research centers like Harvard and Johns Hopkins Universities and the Institute for Educational Leadership have compiled valuable summaries of creative school approaches for building a culture in which families and community organizations are empowered to partner with schools in youth education and development.

Underlying attitudes and strategies for engaging families and community organizations as partners are often missing from preservice teacher training. However, there is universal agreement that support from both community and family increases student achievement, homework completion, in-school behavior, attendance, and high school completion. Parents sense immediately whether they are welcome as partners or are expected to be on call if schools need them. The prevailing culture will determine the extent of their engagement.

Extending Outreach

School leaders often tell me that they plan activities for families but only a few attend. Usually, they blame the parents. At the national family engagement conference, one of the speakers pointed out the fallacy of this thinking as follows: If a movie theater shows a movie and nobody comes, they don't blame the public. They ask why? Was it inadequate marketing? Wrong movie? Comfort of facility? Timing?

All of those questions are valuable for schools as they plan outreach to families and prospective community organizations. Every few years, there will be a turnover of the families who belong to a school, but the school remains a constant fixture in the community. Effective partnerships are formed because school personnel used thoughtfully planned outreach efforts and then made sure that those who came found enough value to come back and spread the word.

Empowering Students

Schools are in business to educate students. School activities should be planned so that family and community partners contribute to students' learning, personal development, and well-being. At the same time, all parties must benefit for a partnership to endure. Activities such as Parent University help build the capacity of families in three ways— helping their children succeed in school, increasing fun activities, and building their own knowledge and skill base.

The U.S. Department of Education released a framework for family engagement called Dual Capacity Building (2015b) noting that effective partnerships will be grounded in efforts that expand the capacity of educators as well as families and community members to contribute to that partnership.

※❁✲❁※

Schools that want to use a systemic approach to inclusion should evaluate their current practices and gather multiple stakeholder perspectives. Does the school have a robust vision and mission that calls all stakeholders to take actions that include and empower all students and all staff? Does the school infrastructure make optimal use of professional strengths and support professional collaboration and learning? Is instruction student centered, utilizing evidence-based approaches, and fostering collaborative classroom learning? Are educators empowered and supported to be effective in their various roles? Are student experiences transition-focused, with opportunities to understand the implications of their disabilities and develop ownership of their own learning? Are stakeholder engagement practices grounded in a welcoming, respectful context that is empowering to families and the surrounding community?

The next step is to create a long-term strategic plan for two or more years incorporating improvements in all five components of inclusion with the students' end of public schooling in mind.

CHAPTER FOUR

LEADERSHIP

Working hard for something we don't care about is called stress; working hard for something we love is called passion.

SIMON SINEK

From my experience from decades spent in education as a teacher, administrator, transition specialist, intern supervisor, and consultant, I have learned that leadership has the single biggest influence on the success of a school. Countless times, I have seen the impact of a new principal on the mood and culture of a school. Teachers either become more unified and collaborative or distrustful and stressed. How schools and districts engage teachers' ownership of new initiatives strongly influences whether teachers will deeply care about new approaches. The priorities for the upcoming school year will determine whether teachers will try new strategies gained in professional development sessions and whether they will persist long enough to gain proficiency. Ultimately, the principal sets the tone for whether school improvement efforts can be achieved and sustained.

The Difference a Principal Makes

When I was the secondary inclusion consultant at the University of Delaware, I facilitated a year-long project called the Student Challenge Initiative in five secondary schools. The intent was to provide support to collaborating teams as they practiced adapting instructional methods for struggling students with learning disabilities in their classrooms. What a difference the principals made!

In each school, I presented the same information about the different types of learning disabilities. I also shared tools for identifying individual student locks on learning based on the work of Gore (2010), scaffolding approaches useful for all students, and ways to measure student growth. By modeling interactive instructional practices, I engaged teachers in all five schools in the same collaborative, problem-solving activities. Then they brainstormed which students they would target for their Student Challenge, formed hypotheses about the specific learning issue to be addressed, and determined which new strategies they would try with those students. I invited them to make specific plans for how they would continue to collaborate between my visits.

In two of those schools, the principals attended my monthly workshops and accompanied me when I conducted classroom walkthroughs. Those two principals reinforced the importance of our initiative by their presence and participation in my sessions. Between my visits they asked teachers how the Student Challenge was going and asked teams to discuss progress at professional learning community meetings. They also looked for evidence of implementation in formal observations. In one of the schools, the principal even invited the teams to share their lessons learned with the whole faculty at an after-school Chili Fest in February and at a Sweet Endings party in June. I gladly attended and contributed my own homemade chili and a pan of brownies.

In the other three schools, the principals waved as I entered the front office, but told me they were too busy that day. I met their teachers without them and provided follow-up coaching on my own. The principals weren't aware of the new vocabulary teachers were learning. They hadn't set any expectations for teachers and didn't hold them accountable. You won't be surprised by the end result.

I was so struck by the differences in the final evaluations, that I presented them at a national conference. Here are a few comments from teachers in the first two schools with principal participation:

- "Learning about brain research as it relates to learning will help me to understand my own students' reactions and needs."

- "I find both students I worked with more open with me and more responsive when I speak to them on an individual basis."

- "I gained the perspective and mindset that I can focus on an individual student and monitor that student's progress in terms of the different learning locks they might have. I also appreciated the brain research about how connecting topics to previous knowledge can help to cement and connect ideas to improve understanding and retention."

- "My team was able to collaborate on specific goals and plans to help an individual student. It was interesting to watch the collaboration when we talked about individual problems. I felt more supported in my job."

In contrast, here are a few comments from teachers in the other three schools without principal participation:

- "This process was absolutely pointless. This was seen as just another task added on top of the eight million things we already have to do."

- "My student showed growth, however, [he] had a run-in with another teacher and felt unsafe. Therefore, he declined and had a difficult time showing growth again. Many plans were implemented but students showed minimal growth."

- "I found the Student Challenge Initiative more of an inconvenience than help. It would've been better for us to have time to collaborate with all the teachers as opposed to learning about the brain."

- "Quite honestly, this initiative was more of a burden than a help to our students. We have so many daily responsibilities that having this dumped on us was an imposition. Teachers involved did not have the time within their contracted day to complete this initiative, as well as completing all of the state and district required mandates."

Do I need to say that principals influence the impact of professional development?

Understanding the Four Aspects of Leadership

There are four aspects of school leadership that are essential to establish a systemic approach to inclusion: (1) vision, (2) culture, (3) infrastructure, and (4) professional learning. When a principal has led the whole school community to craft or revise their written vision statement until it incorporates the values of inclusion, it becomes a call to action. The school culture is determined by routine ways that people interact and respond. These routines may either foster or block effective inclusive practices. Without certain critical supportive infrastructures in place, teachers and students will face needless hurdles in working together to create a positive school culture and actualizing the school vision. Finally, the principal has an influential role in professional learning. As shown in Figure 4.1, these four aspects of leadership need to be in place to optimize inclusive practices.

Figure 4.1

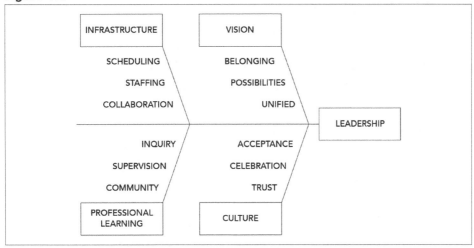

Implementing the Vision

Most schools have a vision statement, but not necessarily current and vibrant. Often, it is posted somewhere in the hall or on the website, but nobody has looked at it in a long time. When I was a SWIFT evaluator, we looked at the vision statement as evidence of the school's inclusive attitude. We looked for wording related to all students belonging and being included. Then we looked for evidence that the school vision translated into action, inspiring both faculty and students to stretch for possibilities. We interviewed faculty, staff, families, and community members to find evidence that they were unified under the vision statement in a common purpose.

It is not enough for a vision to be a cleverly worded statement. It should be regarded as the core of the school improvement plan. The vision statement should also articulate values that are central to school improvement activities and community engagement. This vision should be the beacon that is embraced by students, teachers, staff, and community. Is your school proud of its vision statement?

In my fifth year of teaching English, I attended the fall faculty meeting where we would first greet our new principal, Ken Gahs. My colleagues and I were apprehensive about the changes ahead, but he set the tone for the year in his opening remarks. He said, "You are probably wondering what kind of principal I will be. Well, me too. I've never been a principal before. My plan is to start by listening to you. I'd like to hear what you think is working and what you'd like to see changed." We were all slightly astonished that he would begin his opening remarks to an entire staff by being so candid. He then offered to meet us at the corner bar for the next three Fridays to hear our feedback and take in our perspectives.

True to his word, he showed up to listen. He asked questions, but he didn't control the conversation. The night I went to share, he stayed until the last person was finished talking to him. His actions united us and built relationships that lasted as long as he was principal. With our input, he developed a vision statement and guided us to define how we would achieve it.

In retrospect, I believe that Ken Gahs instinctively understood the change process. Today, school leaders who aren't well versed in change theory are feeling their way in the dark. Reeves (2009) described the following four phases of leading change:

1. Pull the weeds to clear away initiatives that have lost relevance and to create readiness for change.

2. Plan for change that is focused on empowering small, collaborative, group actions. Fullan (2008) calls that process connecting peers with purpose.

3. Support implementation of change with daily conversations to maintain the focus on specific activities to build the targeted instructional culture.

4. Sustain change using a reorientation of priorities and values such that anxiety and fears are replaced by the benefits of the change.

Digging deeper into Reeves' phases can help if change is part of your vision. We will address the change process in more depth in Chapter 12.

Building the School Culture

The school culture is not determined by what is written on the vision statement or by what leaders say—it lives in ways individuals function and interact with each other. If the principal says he values collaboration, but doesn't heed perspectives of teachers or families, there will be a hierarchical power culture. If teachers say they want students to take ownership, but give them no chance to assume responsibility for their own learning, students will continue to be passive learners. If staff members ignore bullying or take no action when students are ostracized, there will be a polarizing culture of those who belong and those who don't.

If you are a principal leading change towards more inclusive practices, you should consider doing a culture assessment. Are there students, faculty, or families that are not accepted into the central life of the school? Are there any members of your school community who believe they or their ideas are not welcome? Is there evidence of bullying or too much focus on students who are discipline referrals? Do your faculty members or families believe that a disability label means low expectations? If so, empower your teacher leaders to investigate ways to shift practices.

Many schools have embraced celebrating positive behavior with Caught You awards. Teachers or students can report someone who was caught in the act of performing a good deed, showing good sportsmanship, or being a friend. At the end of the week, the student is presented with a Caught You award and is recognized by the whole group. This can be expanded to include faculty, family members, and community partners. In schools where teachers face overwhelming challenges, celebration is an antidote to burnout.

One of the least discussed aspects of school culture is trust. Stephen M.R. Covey's book *Speed of Trust* (2006) delineates what it means to trust and be trustworthy. He explains that trust radiates in waves from self-trust into interpersonal trust and then expands to organizational and societal trust. He says, "Simply put, trust means confidence. The opposite of trust—distrust—is suspicion." Nothing dampens school reform like distrust of leadership or leaders' distrust of faculty. Luckily, Covey provides guidelines for examining and building—or rebuilding—trust.

Covey's following four core principles of trust—integrity, intent, capabilities, and results—are useful for our consideration:

- **Integrity** includes speaking honestly, keeping your word, and aligning your actions with your words. If a principal advocates one value, such as inclusion, but his actions don't agree, teachers will lose trust.

- **Intent** has to do with being clear about your agenda. Do leaders interact with respect? Are they open to learning new perspectives that could change their thinking? Do they make it safe for faculty and families to express their opinions? In the end, a principal may need to make some unpopular decisions. Do they explain the reasons behind their decision in a way that clarifies their intent? Do they explain why their choice was the best option?

- To earn the trust of faculty and the community, school leaders will demonstrate that they have the **capabilities** to complete their responsibilities. They are honest about areas where they need help and don't try to disguise their weakest areas.

- Finally, the principal produces **results** in ways that matter. When your school looks at the big picture, has your principal and leadership team produced your targeted results? Are there celebrations and acknowledgement of those who have contributed to that progress?

Creating an Infrastructure

The principal is usually responsible for establishing the infrastructure that underpins all instruction and student-faculty interactions. Inclusive schools have particular structural considerations. How will students with disabilities be dispersed across classrooms in natural proportions? This is a term that means the ratio of students with disabilities in the school will be used to decide how many students with disabilities should be in a typical class. Will all general educators have students with disabilities assigned to them? How will special educators be allocated so that they can most effectively support students and collaborate with a reasonable number of general education partners?

Decisions about scheduling are critical for inclusion. I was recently in a high school where the special educators were assigned as coteachers with multiple general educators in different curriculum areas. Further, they had no common planning period with any of their partners. This was mission impossible! If teachers are scheduled to coteach, they must have scheduled coplanning time. Special educators can also be assigned as learning support coaches for all or part of their day. Learning support coaches are most effective if they have some protected time daily to meet with their assigned students. There are a variety of ways they can be scheduled to collaborate with their general education partners.

To address the needs of all students, not just those with special needs, effective leaders assign teachers to professional teams with specific expectations for collaborating on targeted school issues, such as student progress, curriculum alignment, and teaching strategies. Special educators' expertise should be incorporated into the inquiry and structures of those teams. I cringe when I hear the special educators say they don't have to attend professional teams because they attend IEP meetings. Of course, they are pulled in different directions, but those opportunities to rub elbows with their general educator partners build strong relationships. Incidentally, I've found in my consulting with several schools that workshops focused on building collaboration skills yield immediate results.

Embedding Professional Learning into the Process

The principal is also the leader of professional learning and the one who influences how learning will roll out across the building. Some schools use a professional learning community (PLC) system where teachers gather to examine student data and plan how to meet the needs of students who are struggling. I've seen this method work well as long as teachers are clear about the expectations, know how to interpret data, and have a toolbox of interventions to use. Knowledgeable special educators can be a great resource to the PLC teams.

Another effective model to foster a schoolwide climate of inquiry uses teacher leaders. One school had 20 minutes before school on Wednesdays designated as professional learning time. Four pairs of teacher leaders took on topics that had been identified in their school improvement plan. They split the faculty into four cross-disciplinary groups. Each group met with a teacher leader pair for six weeks before rotating to the next pair. For the first four weeks, the teacher leader pairs introduced relevant learning theory and evidence-based strategies. The process gave teachers a chance to practice and reflect. On the last two weeks, teachers shared how they had used the new approaches in their classrooms, and they provided examples of student work. There was clearly a climate of learning at this school and a camaraderie that was contagious, built from 20 focused minutes each week.

When schools' budgets allow, they invite consultants with specific expertise to evaluate current practices, make recommendations for new approaches, and suggest topics for professional development. From my personal experience, this can be very effective, but only when your school leadership and faculty have clear expectations and plans for supporting the implementation of new practices. After my experience with the five schools described at the beginning of the chapter, I hesitate to provide professional development that doesn't align with overall expectations and support.

Another significant part of professional learning occurs within the appraisal process. During the pre-conference and postconference process, administrators can reinforce their expectations for general and special educator roles in the classroom. They can ask probing questions that will spark new possibilities for collaboration, teacher behavior, and student empowerment.

Recently, I was conducting an initial school tour with a new principal. It was refreshing when he told me that his previous experience did not prepare him to administer or supervise special education. He told me that he was willing to learn, and he trusted me enough to be honest. We used his admission as the entry into several powerful conversations about school vision, culture, infrastructure, and professional learning. You won't be surprised that under his leadership, teachers and students were open to experimentation. The climate of learning was pervasive in that building.

The school principal has tremendous influence over how a school functions and how stakeholders interact. District personnel who empower a school principal and provide needed resources and support are more likely to see improvements that support inclusion and lead to improved post-school outcomes. The four aspects of leadership that are essential to creating a systematic approach to successful inclusion are: creating a vibrant vision of what the school aims to become; a culture of how things are done here that embodies the values of the vision; an infrastructure that supports faculty and students to function effectively; and an ongoing professional learning system that encourages creativity and nurtures faculty growth.

CHAPTER FIVE

PROFESSIONAL COLLABORATION

Unless you listen to my views, accept my right to have views that differ from yours, and take my interests into account, I am unlikely to want to deal with you.

ROGER FISHER AND SCOTT BROWN

In 1970 when I was beginning my career, each teacher was responsible for making independent decisions about what to teach, how to teach, and how to evaluate student learning. A summer committee had decided that our 7th grade English curriculum of basic grammar and reading-writing skills would be organized into the following five literature units: knights and champions, poetry, biography, the outsider, and drama. It was my responsibility to browse through the 7th-grade shelves in the bookroom and decide what my students would read. Of course, I had to negotiate timing with the other three teachers since we only had two class sets of each book.

That was the extent of our collaboration. Being a first-year teacher, I asked the experienced teacher next door for advice, but I didn't have to follow her lead. I had the freedom to decide on my own approach. Similarly, I created my own learning targets and my own unit tests. At first I didn't know where to start. Today, I wonder whether my plans led to rigorous learning. I didn't know anything about using assessments as a basis for instruction or how to evaluate my own teaching. When each teacher made curricular decisions, students definitely had unequal opportunities to learn.

In some ways, as schools have been redesigned, teachers have it easier today. They may complain about their curriculum pacing guides, but at least they know what to teach. Their unit tests are provided by the district or created by a team of grade level teachers. They have opportunities to improve their practice by jointly examining student data to identify student weaknesses and evaluating the effectiveness of their own practice. While those changes have made the job of teaching easier, the demands of collaboration (see Figure 5.1) make the daily life of a teacher much more complicated.

Figure 5.1

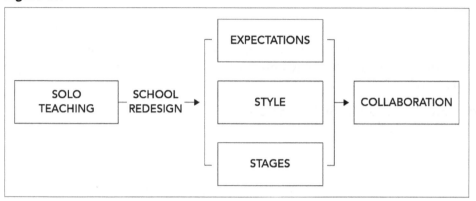

Today, teachers are expected to collaborate with their colleagues in multiple ways. I posed the following question online to middle school teachers: "How many people do you collaborate with regularly?" Their astounding responses are as follows:

- Same-subject content teams meet weekly to agree on curriculum, develop materials, and analyze assessment data.

- Grade-level teams meet weekly to review student progress (e.g., attendance, discipline referrals, grades, or achievement issues) or concerns across all subjects.

- Coteaching teams (e.g., special and general educators) meet daily to plan lesson adaptations for individual students.

- IEP teams (required by special education law) meet for each student with a disability at least annually to review progress, determine needed supports and services, and set annual and post-school goals.

- Behavior intervention teams, including a guidance counselor and behavior interventionist, analyze individual student's problem behaviors and determine, implement, and evaluate intervention plans.

- Committees meet regularly to address topics such as attendance, student activities, field trips, technology, school leadership, sports teams, and family engagement.

Collaboration has become a critical component in education today. I have an entire shelf in my professional library on the topic. My intent is to summarize what it means, what it takes, and how to establish effective collaborative practices. I will focus on the collaboration between general and special educators, but the principles of collaboration apply to all professional collaborative relationships. If we want to achieve greater outcomes for youth with disabilities, professionals must all be included with that end in mind. Collaboration is one way to include all professionals.

Clarifying Expectations About Collaboration

First, let's clarify what we mean by collaboration. I prefer the following definition provided by Friend and Cook (2000)—"Interpersonal collaboration is a style for direct interaction between at least two coequal parties voluntarily engaged in shared decision making as they work towards a common goal." Several terms in this definition are noteworthy. First, this definition specifies why each team was formed—for a common goal. Periodically, it may be useful for team members to realign their purpose, verify that they are working towards the same goal, and confirm that that goal is still relevant.

Notice that collaborative team members are described as voluntary and coequal parties. Sometimes there are circumstances when a school administrator must assign teams, such as hiring new teachers to fill a vacancy, balancing the diversity on a team, or responding to personnel changes over the summer. When possible, I encourage principals to ask teachers their preferences for team assignments. Coequal means that each member has the same status and contributes equally. At times, this may be hard to do when some teachers have more experience and expertise than others, but it is not impossible.

This definition also identifies what happens when collaborative team members meet for direct interaction and shared decision making. In my experience, teachers need specific guidelines to establish routines that will promote those two functions. School leaders committed to expanding the effectiveness of collaborative teams will provide structures for expected practice.

Most of us have little patience for meetings that are a waste of time. I wish I could have back all the hours I've spent sitting in a scheduled meeting where someone made announcements that I could have read or where there was no opportunity for my input. In contrast, I am grateful for all I've learned from collaborative opportunities with colleagues to brainstorm about issues, develop action plans, evaluate progress, and celebrate results. A powerful, effective meeting is exhilarating. The next section shows how school teams will benefit from the following qualities of effective collaboration.

Using Administrative Support

As detailed in Chapter 4, school administrators have a critical role in establishing positive conditions for inclusive collaboration. A principal who establishes new models of inclusion will ensure that every member of the faculty understands the research benefits of inclusion and collaborative teaching. He will also provide professional development and ongoing coaching to support teachers to expand their practice. Equally important, he will create a schedule that makes collaborative teaching possible with scheduling that is conducive to coplanning and coteaching.

Ensuring Commitment

Effective collaboration will not happen unless all teachers commit to doing what it takes to make relationships work. Sometimes veteran teachers appear resistant because they have experienced wave after wave of new initiatives. They want what is best for kids, but have concerns about whether inclusion and coteaching are the best way to go. That attitude is understandable, but it's impossible for me as a consultant to support collaborative coteaching if coteachers haven't committed to make it work. To lay the groundwork, teachers need to understand the justification behind the school's plan for inclusion and buy-in to working as coteachers.

Establishing Effective Communication

Communication, whether it is spoken or written, is a two-way street. Our tendency is to blame the listener for misunderstanding, but if we are communicating, it's up to us to ensure that our message is received. Sometimes others hear our words but not our message. Sometimes they are distracted or focused elsewhere, and don't absorb our meaning. If they are not clear about our intent, they may become defensive, trying to prove that they are right. Miscommunication often leads to misunderstanding, which will undermine collaboration.

I've led a workshop activity that teams find powerful. It's called conditioning the listening, and it focuses on the speaker. Before speaking, articulate your message in one sentence. What do you want them to hear? Then consider your intent. Why do you want them to hear that message? What do you want to accomplish? Finally, imagine how your listener would receive that message. Would he feel attacked or invited to talk? I believe we could deliver almost any message to another person if we establish a context first to make it safe for both the speaker and listener. That context should clarify the intended outcome that you'd like to achieve with your partner. Team members also benefit from exercises that expand their listening skills, including their abilities to restate what they hear to show empathy, reframe negative messages into possibilities, disagree without arguing, read non-verbal messages, acknowledge their partner's contributions, and provide feedback indicating that a message was received.

Setting Aside Time

When a principal tells me that teachers collaborate with one or more teachers, but they have no meeting time scheduled in their professional day, I know what to expect in classrooms. A teacher can't walk into a classroom and ad lib collaborative teaching, especially with a new partner. Planning time every day is ideal, but I've seen special educators with two coteaching partners make it work by meeting once or twice a week with each partner. Highly motivated teachers may meet during lunch or after school, but that wears thin over time. Online tools are helpful as collaborative tools, but they can't substitute for face-to-face time.

Collaborative planning time needs to be protected, too. Teachers sometimes complain to me that they have scheduled collaboration time, but then administrators ask them to cover another teacher's class for an IEP meeting, a field trip, and a doctor's appointment all in the same week. This message conveys that collaboration time isn't important. The bottom line is lack of scheduled planning time equals lack of effective collaborative teaching.

Establishing an Environment for Professionalism

Through their preservice education and student teaching experience, most teachers have assimilated the basics of ethical behavior. There are additional layers of professionalism that accompany working with students with disabilities. For example, teachers seem to be confused about the issue of confidentiality. One morning, after a brief introduction on types of learning disabilities, a teacher approached me to ask if he was allowed to know which students in his class had disabilities. Teachers may need a reminder that confidentiality means that information about a student's individual disability may only be shared with those teachers and staff who work directly with that student. That means teachers are entitled to know about their own students, but may not discuss the students with uninvolved colleagues, curious parents, or fellow students.

In some schools, gossip has a negative impact on school morale. I like the open and fair rule that Murawski and Dieker (2013) promote. Under this rule, faculty members agree that teams will be open in sharing their successes and challenges with other teams, but only if all members of their team are present. Complaining to a colleague about your coteaching partner is a no-no. It's hard to maintain trust without some agreements about professionalism.

Learning How to Problem Solve Together

Most teachers have problem-solving skills needed to function in life. Problem solving as a team is more complex. Teams benefit from using an agreed on framework to approach problem solving. I prefer the following seven-step method from Pugach and Johnson (2002):

1. **Articulate the problem:** Name the dilemma to be solved in general terms as related to students, curriculum, teacher, staff, or building culture. Include a description of the targeted outcome diminished or thwarted by the problem.

2. **Consider contributing factors:** Begin with posing questions (e.g., Who? What? Where? and When?) and then explore all the factors that might contribute to the problem.

3. **Develop a problem-pattern statement:** Summarize the problem and its underlying factors, the group's response to the problem, and a list of controllable areas related to the problem.

4. **Generate solutions:** Brainstorm at least three possible solutions. During brainstorming, groups generate ideas freely without expressing judgment or criticism.

5. **Select solutions:** Empower the individual(s) most directly impacted by the problem to identify the solution most likely to lead to a positive resolution.

6. **Develop an evaluation plan:** Identify a way to monitor the new solution and evaluate whether the intended outcome was achieved.

7. **Implement and monitor the identified solution:** Establish a timeline for implementing and evaluating the effectiveness of the solution. It is important to revisit the problem later to celebrate success or revise a plan that isn't working.

Be certain throughout this process that the teachers experiencing the issue own the problem and the solution. This is especially important when the issue is about student learning and progress, but even more so when it relates to their own collaboration.

Establishing Parity

One mark of effective collaborative partnership is parity, which is defined as "the state or condition of being equal, especially regarding status." How well do both teachers on the team share the work, the responsibility, and the teacher status during instruction?

A first-year teacher once asked my advice. When she met her teaching partner for the first time, he told her that he didn't want special education help. On the first day for students, he announced to the class that he was their teacher and that she was there to help those students with disabilities. Naturally, none of the students would be caught dead talking to her. It was now the second week of school and June looked very far away. What could she do? Undoing that damage was much harder than starting off on a positive note.

If you asked any student in a coteaching classroom, "Who is your teacher?," you would have a good gauge of parity. Students may say things like, "Mrs. Sanchez is my teacher, and Mr. Phillips is her assistant" or "Mr. Johnson is our teacher, and Ms. Kwan helps the slow kids." During August workshops, I tell the story of the first-year teacher and invite them to plan how they will introduce their teaching partner to set the tone for the year.

Parity doesn't mean that both teachers have the same skills. The advantage of collaborative teaching is that teachers with different kinds of expertise can combine their knowledge and skills for the benefit of students. A highly qualified general educator brings knowledge and skills related to a content area; a special educator brings knowledge and skills related to individual differences and scaffolding strategies. I encourage them from the first day to demonstrate to their students that both are teachers capable of leading instruction with the respect and support of the other.

Using Professional Reflection for Growth

Professionals committed to developing their own capabilities as collaborators will take time to reflect on how their partnership is going. They will seek their partner's perspectives and together evaluate ways they can improve. Teachers who have never collaborated effectively before may not know what is possible. They would benefit from professional development that includes structured opportunities to reflect on the components of collaboration listed above. Some principals require all collaborative teams to self-reflect on the effectiveness of their practices and regularly provide updates on their plans for improvement.

Understanding Collaborative Styles

We all like to learn about our favorite subject—ourselves. I enjoy leading a workshop that provides teachers a chance to explore their interpersonal styles. DeBoer (1995) describes four interpersonal styles that are shaped by our emotional hungers, need for structure, willingness to take risks, concrete versus abstract thinking, and people-oriented versus solitary natures. Each style has strengths and approaches to contribute to collaborative situations. Each style also has liabilities and stressors that need to be acknowledged. Each person is a human being with strengths and weaknesses. Knowing each person's collaborative style is valuable as teachers learn to collaborate more effectively. DeBoer describes her four styles as follows:

- **Achievers:** Achievers are natural leaders who are described as chargers, drivers, initiators, and developers. They are self-confident, self-reliant, task focused, and results driven. They prefer interactions to be brief and direct. They aren't focused on feelings. They prefer to concentrate on problem solving and create new approaches to problems. Their liabilities include running over people in efforts to get a job done efficiently. They are often impulsive or impatient without pausing to include others in planning. Their worst fear is losing control of situations if they have authority.

- **Persuaders:** Persuaders are gregarious influencers who combine enthusiastic optimism with imaginative, dramatic communication skills. They inspire others to join efforts through validation of people's self worth. At the same time, they have difficulty managing their time because they focus on others' feelings more than the task at hand. They are often afraid of hurting others. Their worst fears are criticism and disapproval.

- **Supporters:** Supporters are extremely helpful counselors who are concerned about the welfare of others. They can be counted on for moral support and believe that anything worth doing is worth doing well. Before making decisions, they seek a broad range of perspectives by using their strong listening skills. They can ease interpersonal differences and create a cooperative and predictable environment. On the other hand, they resist change and may annoy colleagues by being too nice. Their worst fear is loss of security.

- **Analysts:** Analysts are objective thinkers who are detail oriented, systematic, and disciplined organizers. They thrive on collecting and examining data for evaluative purposes, but they also want to weigh all alternatives and potential outcomes before making any decisions. As a result, they can make valuable contributions to long-term plans. Their liabilities include difficulty making decisions and a concern about doing things the right way. Their worst fear is criticism of their work.

As teachers and administrators learn about these four collaborative styles, they develop an appreciation for the gifts each person brings as well as approaches to use to bring out the best in their teammates. The next step is to encourage teachers to develop specific ways they will use information about styles in their work as instructional partners.

I found this information valuable when I was consulting through the university. I had recruited two retired special education leaders, Karen and Vickie, to work with me as colleagues. We loved to meet informally in Karen's family room to plan workshops. With my laptop connected to her television, all three of us watched our workshop materials unfold as we brainstormed. We were on the edge of our seats by asking questions such as, "What about ...?," "How can we...?," and "What if...?"

I would talk in general terms about the chunks of our workshop, types of activities we could use, and ways we could prompt the participants to practice. Karen would push me to define how long we would spend on each part. She also wanted to pin down the exact wording of the questions we would ask. I felt annoyed that she didn't trust me to use my instinct as an experienced consultant. The day of our workshops, Karen would show up with notecards for her part.

After we learned about collaborative styles, we laughed. I was being an achiever, and she was an analyst. Meanwhile, Vickie, a persuader, was trying to smooth out the friction between us. Understanding the styles helped us understand why we were annoyed with each other. It also gave us vocabulary to smooth the way into communication. I learned to bring a detailed agenda to our meetings. Once Karen saw that there was a specific plan, she could relax and be flexible with how we implemented it. We just needed to allow each other to be different.

Moving Through the Stages of Collaboration

Teachers new to coteaching are relieved to hear that it is normal to grow their collaboration skills over time as they become more comfortable with their partners and become more proficient with strategies and approaches. For many people the journey from solo teaching to collaborative teaching contains unpredictable weather conditions and unexpected road hazards. I advise them to be aware of the interpersonal styles of their partners, make progress in manageable steps, and be gentle with themselves. I've watched entire rooms of teachers exhale when I tell them that they don't have to be masterful the first day. Gately (2005) found that teachers' development of coteaching skills follows three predictable stages.

Navigating the Beginning Stage

When teachers first work with each other they are hampered by not knowing much about their partners as professionals, even if they have known them socially. In addition, they often are unclear about administrative expectations or how to work with each other. I've heard the following statements from teachers in the beginning stage:

- "I don't feel right telling another teacher what to do."

- "I assumed that she knew what to do and would just jump in, but she hasn't."
- "I felt like an invader in his room with no place to put my things."
- "She has more experience in her subject than I do, so I just let her do the teaching."
- "Our principal assigned us as coteachers, but couldn't explain what that means.
- "Sometimes I feel like he's a spy in my classroom, judging my teaching."
- "It was easier to just pull my kids aside to give them what they need."

Administrators who are alert for these signs will reassure teachers and provide professional development with reflective checklists to increase their proficiency. Most of all, they will reinforce the importance of teachers sharing their personal perspectives as critical to moving to the next stage of development.

Moving Into the Compromising Stage

During the second stage, teachers begin to take risks. They may still group students with special needs in certain areas of the classroom to make it easier for the special educator to access them. Frequently, the compromise looks more like taking turns with instruction. While each still has ideas of his or her own way of operating, they are more likely to say things such as

- "I haven't done it that way before, but I'm willing to try his idea."
- "We tried her experiment with grouping students in different ways. "
- "I have let her take the lead in teaching new vocabulary or conducting the review."
- "He is more comfortable letting me step in when students need some clarification."

Notice that each teacher still thinks like a solo teacher, but makes generous attempts to collaborate. Although this is progress, it is still not the best use of two teachers' expertise.

An administrator might challenge them to move to the next stage by asking, "What happened in the room that couldn't have been accomplished with just one teacher?" or "Can you help me justify paying two teachers' salaries for the lesson I just observed?" Posing these kinds of questions without implied criticism will initiate a powerful, open, and reflective discussion.

Coming Together in the Collaborative Stage

Gately (2005) describes the collaborative stage as "Communication is open and interactive and is marked by humor and comfort." In this stage, students with special needs are dispersed throughout the classroom so that they can participate in cooperative-learning activities. Both teachers equally share planning, instructing, grading, and problem solving. Examples of their feedback include the following:

- "It's great how we complement each other. If I move left to provide support to a group, she moves to the center to cover the class. It's like we are dance partners."

- "Because our plans incorporate students with special needs, more of our students succeed."

- "We now determine the key concepts and skills that all students must meet and then adjust expectations for those who are more advanced or behind."

- "We can now read each other's signals and can alter our approach in the middle of a lesson when needed."

- "I love our brainstorming sessions—truly two heads are better than one!"

- "We can experiment with creative approaches to help our students learn because there are two of us to develop the materials."

Often outsiders can't distinguish between the special educator and general educator. Students seek help from both, knowing that both teachers are aligned to give valuable feedback. To reach this level of proficiency, coteaching teams generally need three years and an ongoing commitment to use self-reflection for improvement.

Principals often separate teaching partners too early. Developing strong collaborative skills takes time and practice. As Murawski and Dieker (2013) say, if teachers are starting to dance together, let them dance. If an administrator splits up a team that is still developing their skills at the compromising or early collaborating stage, they will have lost an opportunity to continue learning together.

I worked with one 3rd-grade coteaching team in their second year together. I observed their instruction and provided follow-up coaching each month for a whole school year. They blossomed in their interpersonal skills and their willingness to take risks. By spring, I was videotaping their creative lessons as models for other teachers across the district. In June they shared the devastating news that they would be splitting next year. The general educator would be a solo teacher because the number of incoming 3rd graders with IEPs didn't justify a cotaught class. The special educator would be paired with a 5th-grade teacher whose partner was retiring. I understood those reasons, but what a loss for the teachers, the school, and most of all for the students who wouldn't have the blessings of having them as coteachers. I felt like crying with them.

I understand that a principal has to make tough decisions and sometimes they just can't keep coteaching partners together. But sometimes, they think that if each of these experienced coteachers are combined with someone new, then they'll have two effective coteaching teams. Unfortunately, it doesn't work that way. Now all four teachers have to start from the beginning stage. Partnering a weak teacher with a strong teacher doesn't make a strong coteaching team either. A strong, flourishing coteaching team can mentor other teams on their journey.

The expectations for collaboration have increased in recent years, yet most teachers feel unprepared to partner with other teachers in instructional roles. An effective school leader will ensure that teachers who are assigned to collaborative roles will have appropriate professional development and support. They will clarify their expectations for how teachers will share the instructional load, assume responsibility for the learning of all students, and commit to collaborative improvement.

Teachers benefit from learning about DeBoer's four interpersonal styles, especially as they apply to themselves and their teaching partners. Finally, teachers are reassured to know that their administration will give them needed time and support to progress through the developmental stages of collaboration. School leaders who invest energy and resources to expand collaborative practice report benefits in faculty morale and student learning. Veteran teachers have told me that working with a valued teaching partner renewed their passion for teaching.

CHAPTER SIX

SPECIAL EDUCATION ROLES

Be a lamp, or a lifeboat, or a ladder. Help someone's soul heal. Walk out of your house like a shepherd.

RUMI

I am worried about the plight of secondary special educators today. Too many committed professionals are leaving the field too early and most experience confusion about their roles. The American Institutes for Research (2016) reported that in the 2013-14 school year, 47 states had shortages of special educators. They cited the following three primary reasons leading to the loss of special educators after an average of three to five years:

- **Isolation and lack of shared ownership:** Special educators feel disconnected from other staff who support students with disabilities with disjointed responsibilities.

- **Role ambiguity and less instructional time:** Special educators are overwhelmed by increased legal paperwork and confusion about their instructional value.

- **Lack of leadership support:** Special educators need more support from their instructional leaders who often lack training related to special education best practice.

Administrators tell me they make staff assignments depending on the number of students with IEPs in the school, the number of special educators on staff, and, to a lesser extent, on their training. Regardless of their specific assignment, the following IDEA (2004) standard requires that the intent of their job remains constant:

> ...to ensure that all children with disabilities have available to them a free, appropriate, public education that emphasizes special education and related services designed to meet their unique needs and prepare them for further education, employment, and independent living.

Unfortunately, teachers tell me this purpose statement in the special education law doesn't clarify the specifics of their daily job description. Special educators are expected to provide the following types of services:

- **Accommodations:** Providing alterations to activities, instruction, materials, or classroom environment that do not change the minimal requirements of the task for the purpose of providing access to the general education curriculum.

- **Modifications:** Making substantial changes to products, assessments, or materials that reduce the expectations with instructional level, content, or performance criteria.

- **Instructional supports:** Creating supports and structures that enable a child to learn curricular content, such as focusing attention on important vocabulary and concepts, making relationships concrete, enhancing understanding, and prompting higher order thinking.

- **Behavioral supports:** Providing supports and structures that encourage appropriate behavior and prevent or intervene with problematic behaviors.

- **Case management:** Developing unified coordination of support services provided by teachers, specialists, and families.

While this list helps us to know more about types of special education services, special and general education teachers, as well as administrators, typically want to probe deeper into what special educators do on a daily basis. I still remember on the opening day of a new inclusive high school when a veteran special educator turned to me and said, "If I don't have my own students in my own classroom, what do I do all day?" Together we created the role called Learning Support Coach.

Continuum of Services

IDEA regulations require that students with disabilities have a continuum of placements available to them. This requirement used to be equated with a continuum of settings where students received specialized instruction. Recent research about the benefits of inclusive instruction has reframed our thinking about special education placement options. The spirit of this new thinking views special education as a service, not a place. Unlike when I began as a special educator, receiving special education services doesn't automatically mean being educated in a special education classroom anymore.

During annual reviews, IEP teams are required to determine each student's services and the extent to which those services can be provided in the least restrictive environment. The first consideration is provision of services inside the general education classroom where students can be educated next to their same age peers. In 2014-15, 63% of students with disabilities in the U.S. received their special education services in a general education classroom more than 80% of their day (IDEA, 2015).

When schools request consulting to improve the effectiveness of special educator roles, I help them think through the options, organizing services within a typical comprehensive school into four levels. While many of my colleagues use a variety of terms, I prefer the following labels shown in Figure 6.1 because they make the clearest distinctions based on professional roles: indirect services, learning support coach services, coteaching services, and resource services.

Incidentally, there are more restrictive levels of service outside comprehensive schools, such as separate special education schools, home and hospital instruction,

Figure 6.1

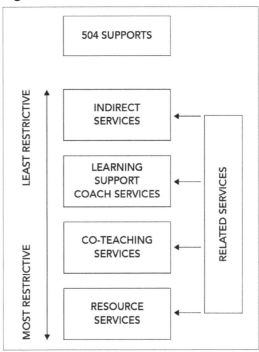

and incarcerated settings. Since this book focuses on inclusion, I will not discuss them here. However, this does not dismiss the important work of those facilities. They are appropriate and valuable for the individuals they serve.

Providing 504 Supports

Some students with disabilities need accommodations that can be provided by a general education teacher without additional services from a special educator. In those cases, support is provided via Section 504 of the *Rehabilitation Act*, rather than under IDEA.

School teams write a 504 plan for those students that describe accommodations they will need to be successful learners. For example, Eric's hearing impairment has not interfered with his grade-level achievement scores. Under his 504 plan, teachers ensure that he has preferential seating away from the noisy heater and remember to face him for speech reading. As long as he continues making progress, he does not need an IEP for special education services.

Implementing Indirect Services

The least restrictive service is within the regular classroom with indirect support of a special educator. In effect, a special educator provides information and technical assistance to the classroom teacher with little direct support to the student. Once the general educator understands the student's disabilities and knows how to provide appropriate accommodations, the student is educated with his nondisabled peers, with progress monitoring provided by the general educator.

Hailey, for example, has a reading disability and needs only indirect services in math class. Her reading comprehension interferes with her achievement when she is faced with reading instructions and word problems, but there are other students in her class who are English language learners. Her math teacher uses strategies suggested by the special educator to support all those who struggle with reading in his class.

Some schools develop an Individual Snapshot IEP updated each year with a brief summary of a student's strengths, support needs, and suggested strategies to share with general educators. In the process of creating each Snapshot, special educators must take care to include the essence of how the student's unique needs impact learning, individualized accommodations and approaches that support achievement, as well as the goals targeted on this year's IEP. School personnel are legally liable for providing the services and supports stipulated on each student's IEP.

I've found that many classroom teachers need orientation to the information on the Individual Snapshot IEPs. Otherwise, they will just tuck them into a folder. After a brief workshop, teachers typically approach me with thanks and say they were uncertain what they were supposed to do with that information before.

Incorporating Learning Support Coach (LSC) Services

The second level of the continuum is occasional special education services, which we named Learning Support Coach services. At this level special educators may be scheduled for specific classes for all or part of a period. They may have the flexibility to decide which class to support based on student and instructional needs. The advantage of the LSC level is that special educator support services can be scheduled more efficiently, especially when budgets limit the number of special educators on staff.

Because the special educator isn't available every period or class, general education teachers and students with special needs can't become dependent on them. Both must develop self-efficacy and self-advocacy skills for teaching and learning. Yet, with effective planning, LSCs can provide extra support during designated learning activities when struggling students may need more intensive instruction and feedback. To reduce the stigma of needing extra help, LSCs provide support to any student in a class, not just those with labels, and call themselves coaches rather than special educators.

I was part of a five-year longitudinal research study of the LSC model at the school where we piloted this model of service delivery. Eisenman, Pleet, Wandry, and McGinley (2010) summarized the three features of the LSC role as follows:

- **Demonstrate caring for the whole student:** Get to know students on the caseload as individuals based on assessment data and a personal relationship; provide coaching on specific skills and background knowledge needed for classroom success (including executive skills such as time management and goal persistence); and mentor use of technology.

- **Communicate frequently with many people:** Establish lines of communication with students, parents, general educators, specialists, and other special educators; employ strong collaborative skills (e.g., trust building, dispute resolution, consensus building, and empowerment).

- **Create a flexibly implemented team approach:** Draw on expertise from both special and general educators and embody an "I've got your back" culture.

Secondary school leaders struggle with organizing this level in a way that provides needed services to students and is manageable for teachers. Generally, it is most effective if special educators are scheduled with a caseload of students on a grade-level, multidisciplinary team. When they provide support to a small caseload of 8-12 students with IEPs, they are able to observe student learning patterns in different classrooms and develop a more holistic view of each student. With their awareness of expectations in each class, they can more effectively foster learning proficiencies with each student.

If a school is not organized into multidisciplinary teams, LSCs can be assigned a caseload of students with IEPs who need specialized instruction across a grade or in one or two subjects. However, the LSCs hired for such positions must have superior organizational skills. It is not an assignment for the faint hearted. Administrators appreciate the following reminders for scheduling and supporting the work of LSCs:

- **Maintain natural proportions:** Natural proportions ensure that students with disabilities and others who may need intensive support (e.g., English language learners, students with 504 plans, and other at-risk learners) are not the majority of the class.

- **Schedule regular meetings:** Ensure that each LSC has scheduled time daily to meet with his or her caseload of students to reinforce self-determination skills.

- **Establish routines for collaboration:** Encourage LSCs and general educators to establish routines for collaboration. Some LSCs attend content-based PLCs to stay current with unit expectations. In the school we studied, general educators respected the pedagogical expertise of LSCs and frequently sought their advice for structuring challenging material.

It's not an accident that we decided to use the term coach. A coach builds a trusting relationship with someone who is committed to expanding skills in a specific domain (e.g., tennis, financial success, literacy, or relationships). A powerful coach envisions possibilities for that individual's evolution and guides him to expand competencies to become more proficient. The coach is able to anticipate breakdowns and encourages the individual's self-reflection as he meets each challenge.

Incorporating Coteaching Services

Based on an IEP team decision, some students will succeed in a general education classroom with support of a special educator to provide specialized instruction most of the time. These students may need more scaffolding, guided practice, feedback, or one-on-one support for academics or behavior.

For example, the IEP team may determine that one student, Raj, needs coteaching supports in English and social studies because of a reading disability. But he could function quite well with LSC services or indirect services in his other classes because he is quite gifted in math and has developed an extensive background in science. On the other hand, the team may decide that another student, Alicia, needs coteaching support for all four academic classes because her attention deficit hyperactivity disorder manifests with major cognitive and physical disorganization.

Scheduling Coteaching. In my experience, the effectiveness of coteaching hinges on strategic scheduling and the effectiveness of collaboration. Administrators grapple with questions, such as, "How many partners should a coteacher have?" and "Should special educators coteach in only one subject?" The answer is "It depends." These factors are dependent on the competencies and comfort level of all the partners. Nobody should be assigned to coteach unless they also have a protected coplanning period with that teacher at least once per week. If you can't plan, you can't coteach.

It is often effective to schedule special educators as coteachers for just part of their day. For example, here are some possible coteaching configurations for special educators that I have seen effectively implemented.

- Aliesha coteaches with a U.S. history teacher for two classes a day. They each have only one coteaching partner and have a coplanning period nearly every day. They thrive from opportunities to discuss and adjust each lesson before teaching it to their second class later in the day.

- Randolph coteaches with two 8th-grade math teachers in the morning and in the afternoon. All three meet together for coplanning twice a week. They each contribute to developing materials and brainstorm instructional approaches that have universal appeal to diverse students.

- Vienna coteaches with a math teacher in the morning and a science teacher in the afternoon. Although these are two different content areas, it works well because she is working with the same 6th-grade students in both classes. During her coplanning sessions, she can bring a broader view of students' functioning.

Other configurations can work if they have been strategically planned with the teachers' personalities and competencies in mind and time has been allocated for coplanning. Asking teachers to find time after school or during their lunch break will not work in the long run.

Planning for Coteaching. We have also learned the hard way that simply allocating time for coplanning is insufficient. Schools with effective coplanning have invested in professional development and ongoing support for teachers to develop their collaborative skills.

During inclusion rounds in one school, I was invited to observe several pairs of teachers during their coplanning sessions. I was dismayed to see that in one classroom the social studies teacher did most of the talking. She explained her plans to introduce vocabulary, have students read a chapter, and then have students complete a summary worksheet. The special educator nodded, took notes, and said, "OK, I'll be ready." She didn't say, "What about scaffolding?," "What about universal design?," or "What about student engagement or collaborative learning?" Yet, I knew she had skills in all those areas.

In the second planning session I observed, two teachers spent at least 20 minutes complaining about how out of control their class was. This is called admiring the problem. The special educator turned to me with raised eyebrows, "Do you see how impossible our job is? You wouldn't believe the homes these kids come from." They had given up before the year had barely begun. I wanted to talk with them about Carol Dweck's (2006) concept of fixed mindsets where someone believes ability is fixed at birth and can't be changed. These teachers certainly had a fixed mindset about their class.

To make optimal use of coplanning time, coteachers could share lesson plans on an online platform, such as Google documents, shared calendars, or wikis. The general educators can post lesson elements like common core objectives and rigorous curricular content ahead of time. This gives special educators time to consider ways to adjust the content, expand options, or include activities that will address needs of individual students and engage more learners.

The most effective coplanning occurs when teachers structure their planning sessions. Here's an example of a typical coplanning agenda if teachers have been able to prepare prior to the meeting:

5 min:	Review unit and lesson objectives and student outcomes
10 min:	Review and plan summative assessment expectations and options
10 min:	Plan instructional activities and formative checks
10 min:	Discuss individual student concerns
5 min:	Agree on next steps and responsibilities
5 min:	Reflect on status of collaboration
45 min	**Total**

Of course, teachers have the freedom to flex their time on each topic, as long as they hit each topic during every session. In schools where this is most effective, the principal expects teachers to report regularly on their coplanning sessions.

Establishing Coteaching Structures. Coteachers have a variety of instructional structures they can use. I usually suggest that they begin with the one or two they find most comfortable. Both students and teachers are enlivened with variety, so the more they use, the better. I encourage teachers to aim for using two or three structures during each day's lesson, especially if they work in a block schedule of 90-minute periods.

Here are the seven coteaching structures I include in my workshops. Note that I've expanded the five structures that are usually described by Villa, Thousand, and Nevin (2008):

1. **One teach-One support:** One teacher takes the lead during teacher-centered instruction and the other teacher assumes responsibility for supportive instructional tasks, such as asking clarifying questions, inviting students to summarize, and modeling note taking.

2. **Parallel teaching:** Each teacher instructs half the class (usually heterogeneous groups) on the same learning objective, with different approaches.

3. **Alternative teaching:** One teacher instructs most of the class, and the other teacher provides remediation, previewing, or enrichment to a small, homogeneous group.

4. **Station teaching:** Both teachers facilitate learning as students rotate to stations focused on a specific skill or chunk of content.

5. **Shared facilitation:** Both teachers facilitate student practice, support cooperative learning, and provide individual and small-group feedback.

6. **One teach-One observe:** While one teacher takes primary responsibility for instruction, the other teacher collects data on a specific student or the class as a whole to be used in evaluating progress and teaching effectiveness.

7. **Team teaching:** Both teachers share instruction together, employing equal responsibility for a variety of roles.

Providing Resource Services

As schools become more comfortable with designing instruction and scaffolding for more diverse students, fewer students are pulled aside for separate instruction. Yet, some students may have intensive resource services for remedial, functional, or empowerment needs. These services are provided with a small student-teacher ratio.

For example, I visited a school that is very successful including students with high-functioning autism, sometimes known as Asperger's Syndrome. For 45 minutes each day, the 9th graders meet with Ms. Spangler, the autism specialist, who also provides LSC services in their classes. The day I dropped by, they were talking about an incident in their morning class.

Jason had become alarmed when he noticed a classmate texting under her desk. He shouted, "Shelby is breaking the rules!" In the safe space of the resource classroom, Ms. Spangler reminded the class that students on the autism spectrum often view the world as black and white, right and wrong. They talked about the hard decisions of fitting in socially versus doing the right thing. She invited them to suggest other ways Jason might have handled his outrage instead of tattling. This was a safe environment for such a discussion and prepared students to be more successful in the general education classroom.

Some students may have significant weaknesses in academic skills that require modified materials and expectations. Many resource programs address Common Core State Standards through a functional, real-life curriculum that is designed to prepare these students to be successful in adult life. Many advocates believe that students, regardless of the severity of their disability, should have all their services provided in the general education classroom. Brain researchers are discovering instructional methods that will revolutionize how students with moderate and severe disabilities can learn. Until they have translated their research findings into classroom practice, I believe some students will continue to receive intensive, focused, specialized instruction in a small-group setting for part of their day.

Sometimes, it is easier to describe what resource services should not be. A few years ago a principal took me to a science classroom for life-skills students. The teacher told her students to pay attention to a video about marine life and then color a picture of an octopus. The principal said to me, "I don't think that should be going on, but I don't know what I should expect." Students receiving resource services should be receiving highly individualized and specialized instruction that is designed to remediate or teach them to compensate for gaps in their knowledge and skills. Many successful programs teach the standards within a context for transition to real-life functioning.

Embedding Related Services
In addition to the supports provided by special and general educators, many students receive other related services. Guidance counselors, psychologists, nurses, social workers, and behavior specialists have responsibilities to all students in the school, including those students with disabilities. Other specialists, including speech-language pathologists, physical and occupational therapists, and vision-hearing specialists, are hired with special education funding. They provide evaluations that contribute to determining eligibility for special education services. They also provide individualized services as specified on a student's IEP.

Until recently, most of these related services were provided in a pullout model. Teachers were concerned about out-of-class time for the students who also needed the most exposure to strong instruction. Today, these services are more likely to be embedded into regular instruction, such as speech therapy within vocabulary practice and physical therapy within physical education.

Paraprofessionals are the unsung heroes of special education services. With appropriate preparation for their roles and effective communication with both special education and general education teachers, they can provide small-group support, one-on-one support, and coaching to students with disabilities. It is critical that they understand the difference between enabling and empowerment so that students develop self-reliant skills, not dependency.

Professional roles have evolved with the advancement of inclusion. The decisions made by administrators about teaching assignments and scheduling are critical to the effectiveness of special educators. IEP teams determine appropriate levels of services for each student with a disability based on individual strengths and needs in each content area. I organize those services into the following continuum from least to most restrictive—504 services, indirect services, LSC services, coteaching services, and resource services. Push-in related services and paraprofessional support are also incorporated into classroom instruction.

CHAPTER SEVEN

INSTRUCTION: LEARNING TO LEARN

There is a special talent locked in the mind of the unusual learner. The trick is to unlock it.

JONATHAN MOONEY

Professional libraries are bulging with resources on instructional methodologies that address the needs of students with and without disabilities. My office shelves are stacked with books that I value for their approaches. I have used them as a foundation for graduate courses and professional development sessions. I respect those authors who grounded their work in the latest educational theories, published research, and their own experiences in the field.

However, over the last decade, I have become disillusioned with some of those approaches. Maybe it's because I've come down from the Ivory Tower and now spend more time out in the trenches. Repeatedly, I am struck by the disconnection between rhetoric about school improvement and the lack of true learning going on in classrooms today. Advocates calling for school reform are increasing the pressure on schools to perform. That pressure is felt by administrators and teachers in the classroom. I see them frantically scrambling to do more. I also see increasing burnout and frustration. I have found a few pockets of amazing excellence, but I don't see much large-scale improvement in teaching or learning.

In my perpetual search for glimmers of hope, I have uncovered publications that could transform teachers' practices based on groundbreaking research and evidence. However, I worry that these new practices will be dumped on teachers in one-size-fits-all professional development sessions, and teachers who are already overwhelmed will be left to integrate it all into a system that makes sense for them. Most teachers won't go through that process. They are too busy managing urgent responsibilities to take on anything else. More than ever before, teachers and school leaders need a unified, focused, manageable system for instruction that leads to satisfying outcomes with their students.

Student-Centered Learning

Fundamentally, the new approach that I'm advocating has student-centered learning at the heart. The term keeps appearing in school reform rhetoric, but when I have spoken with teachers and leaders in public schools, I've found little evidence of understanding or practice. Our teacher-centered modes of instruction are so entrenched that it's hard for teachers to conceive of doing things any other way.

When I was a student in the 1950s and 1960s, schools were clearly teacher-centered. The point of education at that time was to cram our heads full of facts and information. I was a *B* student, which meant I was above average in my ability to retain and recite information. I spent hours reading, memorizing dates, and doing flash card drills so I could be one of those good students. I often found myself squirming if my teachers talked for too long. It was hard to memorize complicated masses of information.

In English, I was good at remembering details of setting and characters in a story. I was a wiz at grammar and diagramming sentences. Thinking that this was a natural gift, I became an English teacher. I ruled out being a scientist without a second thought. After all, I had bought the cultural bias that girls could only be teachers, nurses, and secretaries.

My grade in science provided more evidence. I was short for my age and invisible behind the last lab desk. I had been assigned there because my last name was near the end of the alphabet. My teacher, Mr. Jennings, didn't write on the chalkboard, and we had no lab manuals. Instead his voice came from somewhere behind his massive demonstration counter, rattling off the steps of our next experiment. I could barely see or hear him so I spaced out. Luckily, Andy, my lab partner, was taller and good at science. He could assemble the equipment and recall how to conduct the experiment. I just needed to follow his lead to avoid total failure.

If there had been a special education law then, I wonder if I might have been given a disability label based on my achievement in science class. But was the problem with me or with Mr. Jennings' instruction? I wonder about all the youth over the years who found school a place where they couldn't succeed. I wonder what decisions they made about their own competencies and their future. If they decided that they couldn't learn, I wonder if they found an Andy to tag after, became behavior problems, or simply dropped out of school.

We are all familiar with traditional, teacher-centered instruction that I perpetuated with my graduate students. Teachers assign textbook chapters, lecture, show a movie, and arrange group discussions about the topics. Good teachers provide students with a checklist or graphic organizer for developing their projects and a rubric listing criteria for a passing grade. Better teachers provide guidance and feedback along the way to support students learning the targeted knowledge and skills. The best teachers give students opportunities to expand their thinking skills through structured, collaborative learning.

When final tests or projects are submitted, teachers assign each student a grade. Once grades are posted, what can teachers do for students who failed? Can they isolate the knowledge or skill gaps for each student? Teachers tell me that sometimes they can pinpoint the problems with a student's achievement, but they don't see how to provide remediation without having him fall further behind the class. More students than we'd like to admit would give up along the way and miss out on possibilities of becoming expert learners. In the end, most teachers just move on to the next unit. I don't blame them. When you don't know what to do, it's easier to keep doing what you know.

Special education requires that we adapt instruction for those students with IEPs. Respected experts describe methods for individualizing instruction to meet the needs of each disabled student. These experts also recommend that teachers differentiate the content, process, and products of instruction to address learning differences of groups within the classroom. I've led workshops for teachers modeling how to individualize and differentiate based on those theories, and I generally get the following response from teachers. "That's all fine. I agree that it *should* be done, but with my teaching responsibilities, I just don't have the time or resources to implement either individualization or differentiation on a daily basis."

If the task of individualizing or differentiating for each student's needs is assigned to the general or special education teacher, it becomes a daunting task and is still teacher-centered instruction. What if, instead, we empowered all students to take ownership for their own learning and gave them tools so that they could do their own individualizing and differentiating? In student-centered instruction, educators design flexible educational experiences and empower each learner to adjust the specifics of the content and tasks to fit their own needs whether they have a label or not.

Teachers say, "I've tried student-centered learning, but my students aren't motivated." Deci and Ryan (2002) provide useful key vocabulary so we can ask if students are **amotivated** (i.e., not having motivation or just going through the motions) or **motivated** (i.e., having intentionality and a desire to accomplish some outcome). Further, are they **autonomous** (i.e., demonstrating actions that are freely pursued and wholly self-endorsed) or **controlled** (i.e., no choice due to external or internal forces)? All people—both students and educators—have an innate desire to be causal agents in their own lives.

In student-centered instruction, the question is not whether students are motivated, but whether they have intrinsic motivation (i.e., responding to internal forces) rather than extrinsic motivation (i.e., responding to external rewards or punishment). Numerous studies investigated the short- and long-term impact of giving students rewards for tasks. While rewards may increase the likelihood that they will complete tasks initially, researchers found that in the long run, students who were given external rewards became less intrinsically motivated to achieve (Deci & Ryan, 2002).

Deci and Ryan (2002) also emphasize the importance of the relationship between the adult and student in building intrinsic motivation. They say, "Using an autonomy-supportive style, adults accept that a student might find the material boring or that it is not optimal for his or her skill level, and then the adults might explain why the material is important or they might adjust the difficulty level, as seems appropriate at the time being responsive to the student rather than simply being demanding of him or her." They state that adults can increase student's intrinsic motivation through praise that a task was finished completely and autonomously, thereby promoting their perceived causality. An example would be acknowledging a student for making the choice to assume responsibility for an assignment when she could have chosen not to complete her work.

Intrinsic motivation is enhanced through giving students voice in their learning, a cornerstone of student-centered instruction. The description of student-centered instruction that I find most helpful is based on the interaction between the teacher and student. Neumann (2013) makes the following three distinctions to clarify the contours of student-centered instruction:

- **Centered in students** assumes that we are all natural learners who come with our own curiosity and quest for understanding. Anyone who has been subjected to a three year old's incessant questioning knows this to be true. If learning is centered in students, teachers will facilitate their inquiry and get out of their way. Montessori schools are based on learning centered in students.

- **Centered on students** is more commonly implemented in schools. Teachers provide a range of curricular frameworks and externally prescribed learning goals. Students are provided choices about how they will pursue those goals and are guided to reach the outcomes determined by the teacher. Students can make selections, but have little freedom to pursue their own independent learning within school walls. Students who succeed tend to be compliant in managing ready-made knowledge rather than developing initiative, efficacy, and intrinsic motivation.

- **Centered with students** emphasizes a partnership between teachers and students. Based on a respect for students as autonomous learners, teachers "enlist students in a more reciprocal learning relationship."

Citing the work of John Dewey to further explain learning centered with students, Neumann (2013) says,

> In this collaboration, Dewey does not allow students free rein in pursuit of their desire to become more fully acquainted with their surroundings. Nor, on the other hand, is the tutor or teacher to have free rein in determining what students will do and how they will do it.

In this third contour of learning, teachers and students together make contracts and agreements for what students will learn based on students' interests and preferences for content and method. They would also collaborate on determining the methods used to evaluate progress and criteria for mastery and incorporate ways for the teacher to provide ongoing feedback and guidance.

Neumann (2013) acknowledges two difficulties faced by any teacher wanting to implement learning centered with students in a public school today. First, curriculum is heavily influenced by externally determined, standardized expectations that reduce teachers' freedom to jointly design learning with their students. Second, given our current system of required high school credits for graduation (e.g. 4 English, 4 math, 3 social sciences, 2 world language, etc.), what can you do if your students aren't interested in a required subject?

While I think the most empowering approach is the third contour, centered with students, I also believe that most teachers and students in secondary comprehensive schools are not ready yet for such a paradigm shift.

Game Changing Influences

In Figure 7.1, I have identified seven key influences on school transformation that bring potential challenges and exciting possibilities for school transformation. Our custom has been to provide separate professional development workshops on each new approach and hope that teachers will figure out how to integrate them in daily

Figure 7.1

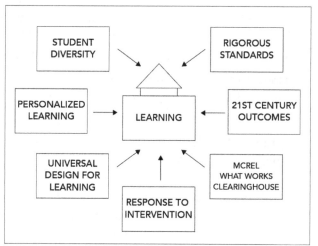

practice. Instead, I propose to discuss these seven current influences and then suggest five integrated principles to guide teachers' implementation.

Embracing Student Diversity

Teachers complain to me that when they plan lessons for the average student, they don't know how to meet the needs of those who struggle and those who excel. Todd Rose's TED Talk (2013) describes this "myth of average," and warns about the dangers of instruction for the average student.

The reality is that the population of our public schools is increasingly diverse. An inclusive classroom today will have students with disabilities, English language learners, and students living in poverty or homeless. These new faces bring a spectrum of previous experiences and needs into the classroom. Each learner comes with different background knowledge, different personality traits, and different ways of processing information.

John King, Acting Secretary of the U.S. Department of Education (2016), urged schools to encourage children with a range of ethnicities, linguistic proficiency, and socioeconomic status to pursue careers in education to meet the growing demand for diversity in the teaching professional. Teachers today can't ignore the spectrum of students in their classrooms. Addressing these individual differences will strongly influence how they plan instruction.

Implementing Rigorous Standards

Much has been written about the Common Core State Standards for literacy and math, which were adopted by 42 states as of 2013. The passage of *Every Student Succeeds Act* (ESSA) of 2015 was a response to the controversy of the federal government's role in determining standardized outcomes for education. With ESSA, the power to set and evaluate standards is returned to states.

Regardless of your perspective, having new rigorous standards changed what happens in classrooms, especially those with diverse populations. Teachers can no longer decide that some students aren't capable of grade-level standards. Teachers no longer have permission to water down the curriculum. As a result, more students are being exposed to more challenging content. More students are expected to develop higher order thinking skills. Teachers must base their lessons on challenging, rigorous standards, but often are unclear about how to do that in view of the diversity in their classrooms.

Producing 21st-Century Outcomes

Businessmen and public officials have become increasingly concerned about the status of public education in this country, with good reason. Student achievement has shown a downward trend in most measures. In 2015 the Organization for Economic Cooperation and Development announced that 15 year olds in the U.S. ranked 29th in the world in math and science achievement (Coughlan, 2015).

Since their founding in 2002, the Partnership for 21st Century Learning (P21) has gained momentum as a coalition of like-minded organizations to kick-start a national conversation that would identify and promote the importance of 21st-century skills for all students. The P21 website (2015) describes their purpose as follows: "Representing over five million members of the global workforce, P21 unites business, government and education leaders from the U.S. and abroad to advance evidence-based education policy and practice and to make innovative teaching and learning a reality for all."

The P21 framework encourages educational institutions to address the following 21st-century student outcomes:

- **Key subjects** (e.g., English, reading, world languages, arts, mathematics, and social sciences) and interdisciplinary themes (e.g., global awareness; financial, economic, business and entrepreneurial literacy; civic literacy; health literacy; and environmental literacy)

- **Learning and innovation skills** (e.g., creativity and innovation, critical thinking and problem solving, communication, and collaboration)

- **Information, media, and technology skills** (e.g., information literacy— the ability to access, evaluate, use, and manage information and media)

- **Life and career skills** (e.g., flexibility and adaptability, initiative and self direction, social and cross-cultural skills, productivity and accountability, and leadership and responsibility)

The P21 Outcomes go beyond the academic rigor of the Common Core State Standards to encompass skills that all students will need for adult settings. If youth with disabilities are included in opportunities to develop these 21st-century proficiencies, they will be more prepared for their transition into adulthood. How can teachers incorporate these skills into their lessons?

Incorporating Research from the McREL What Works Clearinghouse

The federally funded Mid-continent Research for Education and Learning Center (McREL) has made substantial contributions to education. Their staff reviews and categorizes the findings of published studies and prepares summaries of instructional strategies that meet quality research criteria. In their What Works publications, Dean, Hubbell, Pitler, and Stone (2012) announced the following nine categories of instructional strategies that increase student achievement:

- Setting objectives and providing feedback
- Reinforcing effort and providing recognition
- Using cooperative learning
- Using cues, questions, and advance organizers
- Incorporating nonlinguistic representations
- Summarizing and note taking
- Assigning homework and providing practice
- Identifying similarities and differences
- Generating and testing hypotheses

McREL asserts that these instructional strategies are "'best bets' for developing 21st-century learners because they help students set personal learning goals, self-check for understanding, access tools and resources for enhancing their understanding, and use what they have learned in real-world contexts" (Dean, Hubbell, Pitler, & Stone, 2012). I've seen teachers who learn to use these strategies within their routine instructional practices discover that students gain higher levels of mastery.

Using RTI

The federal government has funded a center to support states, districts, and schools with implementing Response to Intervention (RTI). The National Center on Response to Intervention (2010) defines RTI as "integrat[ing] assessment and intervention within a multi-level prevention system to maximize student achievement and reduce behavior problems."

There is strong evidence that when schools embed the following four components of RTI into their routine practices, there are increases in student learning and decreases in behavior problems. These practices are as follows:

- **Multi-level prevention system:** Students are provided interventions to prevent school failure organized into a multi-tiered system of support (MTSS), sometimes called Tier I, Tier II, and Tier III.

- **Universal screening:** Schools have a system for screening all students to identify those students who are at risk for poor learning outcomes.

- **Progress monitoring:** Schools have a system for monitoring student progress and the effectiveness of supports provided to students.

- **Data-based decision making:** Teachers use data to make decisions about students' movement within the tiers of support, the extent of students' progress, and the improvement of instructional quality.

Elementary schools have been using RTI for over a decade. The practices have spread to secondary schools as methods for measuring growth have become more available. It's exciting to work with teaching teams as they analyze data to monitor the effectiveness of their interventions and celebrate student growth.

Applying Universal Design for Learning

The Center for Applied Special Technology (CAST) began in 2002 as a center that adapted books and education materials for students with disabilities referred to their center. Later, CAST (2014) declared that "the curriculum, rather than the learners, was the problem," and changed their direction. They also said:

> ...our future lay not in helping students overcome the barriers they found there but in helping schools and educators to lower or eliminate those barriers. In the future that we imagined, more students would thrive in their schools and fewer students would have to be ... labeled 'patients.' The new technologies could go beyond changing students. They could change schools.

CAST developed a framework for instruction of diverse learners called Universal Design for Learning (UDL). The UDL framework is based on the work of neuroscientists who view the brain "as a complex web of integrated and overlapping networks.... learning is seen as changes in the connections within and between these networks" (Meyer, Rose, & Gordon, 2014). Their framework includes the following three principles that tap into the primary neurological networks:

- **Multiple means of engagement:** This principle includes recruiting students' interest, supporting them to develop persistence and monitor their performance with their affective brain networks.

- **Multiple means of representation:** This principle includes providing a variety of ways for learners to access information and learning. It also draws on text and multimedia resources so that students' recognition brain networks can recognize and make meaning from new information.

- **Multiple means of action and expression:** This principle includes offering students opportunities to use their strategic brain networks to plan, organize, and initiate purposeful actions.

For student-centered instruction, we also need to redefine what we mean by learning. Everyone today agrees that learning is much more than memorizing facts. Meyer and colleagues (2014) define learning as "the dynamic interaction of the individual with the environment or context." The UDL framework states that the purpose of education is to make expert learners, not ones who merely "pass the class." They define expert learners as ones who are "purposeful/ motivated, resourceful/ knowledgeable, and strategic/ goal-directed."

The 2015 reauthorization of ESSA encourages states to implement UDL principles within instructional strategies to reach diverse learners, especially within their literacy comprehensive plans. Further, it encourages them to adhere to UDL within student assessments and grants permission to use federal funding for technology needed for UDL.

I believe that UDL opens possibilities for including all students in learning opportunities. Picture classrooms where teachers and students together design how they will approach learning, what adaptations they will need, and how they will demonstrate their mastery. In these classrooms, teachers' efforts can be directed towards coaching students through tough spots rather than persuading students to "pay attention." How rewarding for teachers, and what an exciting world for teenagers!

Promoting Personalized Learning

In addition to UDL, Blad (2016) reports that the new ESSA provisions also encourage states to pursue personalized learning models. Personalized learning is a relatively new term for practice of UDL in classes or across a whole school. Most of us can think of a time when we have become personally interested in a topic and have expanded our knowledge and skills without extrinsic motivation or reward. Schools that adopt models of personalized learning give students voice and choice about their learning experiences and find that students come alive as learners.

I prefer the definition of personalized learning from the Institute for Personalized Learning:

> Personalized learning is an approach to learning and instruction that is designed around individual learner readiness, strengths, needs and interests. Learners are active participants in setting goals, planning learning paths, tracking progress and determining how learning will be demonstrated. As such, learning objectives, content, method and pacing are likely to vary from learner to learner. A fully personalized environment moves beyond both differentiation and individualization. (Rickabaugh, 2016).

I recommend that schools wanting to make learning more personal for students also investigate the websites of the Innovative Schools Network and Personalize Learning, LLC. Bray and McClaskey's (2014) publications provide organizational frameworks based on their research of personalized learning in this country and abroad. They report that in personalized learning environments each learner "demonstrates mastery of content in a competency-based system" and "becomes a self-directed, expert learner who monitors progress and reflects on learning based on mastery of content and skills." They provide guidance in three stages of development for schools as they move forward to embrace personalized learning.

Developing an Integrated Approach to Instruction

The ESSA 2015 has set an ambitious goal. It declares that the purpose of education is "to provide all children significant opportunity to receive a fair, equitable, and high-quality education, and to close educational achievement gaps." How can we do that?

Figure 7.2

I propose an integrated approach that teachers can use to plan instruction based on five tenets. As depicted in Figure 7.2, these tenets appear to be sequential, but in fact, the boundaries between them are blurry. Decisions made under each tenet will influence and alter how teachers and students operate across the whole learning process. I have separated them as tenets to provide a practical systems approach for teachers that integrate all seven of the influences described above.

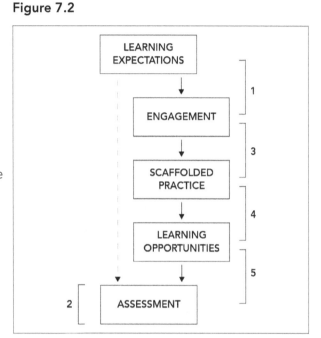

I recommend that teachers use this framework to create a template for instruction that they can adjust for each unit throughout the school year. Collaborating teachers will want to design their template together and use the five tenets framework as a basis for evaluating their progress with students as well as with each other.

For clarity, I will illustrate the steps using a five-day, middle school U.S. history sample lesson plan. I will describe how I would organize my instruction as a solo teacher responsible for diverse learners. I will also include possibilities for effectiveness that include support from a second adult, such as a special educator, English language learner specialist, related services therapist, or a paraprofessional.

Tenet 1. Setting Learning Expectations

Key question: What do I want my students to know and be able to do?

In a fully personalized learning environment, students review lists of standards and make decisions about their learning expectations with the support of a teacher mentor. Since most units and lessons in schools today begin with an externally established standard, and teachers create learning choices for student-centered learning, I will use the following standard for my sample lesson:

> Compare the point of view of two authors for how they treat the same topic, including which details they include and emphasize in their respective accounts. (adapted from CCSS.Literacy, Grade 9-10>6).

Once the standard is identified, the teacher's work of task analysis begins. For this example, I decided to incorporate the stated standard in my U.S. history unit on the Civil War. I want my students to understand northern and southern perspectives leading to the Civil War, so I'll reframe two authors as two perspectives. I must look deeper to itemize the embedded expectations for how the standard will play out in my lesson. Many teachers find collaborating with another teacher during this stage is especially beneficial. By the end of this lesson, my students will be able to:

Knowledge expectations:

- Describe the role of slavery in the economy of the South.
  (Bloom's understanding level)

- Explain reasons for northern opposition to slavery.
  (Bloom's understanding level)

Skill expectations:

- Identify point of view and perspectives of authors in text.
  (Bloom's understanding level)

- Select details in the text that authors use to support their claims.
  (Bloom's evaluating level)

- Develop a comparison-contrast essay.
  (Bloom's analyzing and creating levels)

I have tagged each expectation with a Bloom's Taxonomy category (Overbaugh & Schultz, n.d.). This is a useful way to ensure that my expectations will push my students to learn new vocabulary, concepts, and skills at the simplest level (i.e., remembering and understanding) and then apply them using more complex thinking (i.e., applying, analyzing, evaluating, and creating).

Tenet 2. Assessment

Key question: What are the ways that my students could show evidence that they have mastered the expectations for this lesson? How can we monitor their progress along the way?

I will imagine some summative assessment options so my students and I can evaluate whether they achieved the lesson expectations. Since I am committed to student centered learning, I would give students the following range of choices for their final products:

- Write a comparison essay
- Create an illustrated multimedia presentation or poster
- Orally describe the differences between the two perspectives to a teacher or peer group using an organizer you develop
- Prepare videotaped interviews with real or fictional characters
- Create your own design

I would guide students to consider each option and decide on a learning path that would draw on their strengths while developing the skills that we have identified jointly. Students would be clear from my evaluative rubric that regardless of the medium they choose, their summative products will reveal their understanding of the historic, divisive perspectives of the North and South on slavery, economic growth, and governmental power that led to the Civil War and demonstrate their skills of developing a comparison composition.

Since my goal is to have all my students reach proficiency, in addition to the summative assessment, we will plan benchmarks along the way so that students can monitor their own progress and gain peer feedback. In addition, both I and my students will use multiple formative assessment measures for feedback about progress and to realign with learning targets and guide their revisions. Formative assessment data will include a mix of my professional observations, notes from individual check-ins, and student-submitted reflective progress reports. I will adjust my interactions with students and resources I make available in response to these data.

Assuming that my school has embraced RTI, I am aware of how each of my students has scored on our universal literacy screening. Whether they have a disability label or not, I know which students participate in Tier II or Tier III interventions and will monitor their progress accordingly. If feasible, I will collaborate with the instructors responsible for RTI interventions so they can reinforce learning targeted in this lesson.

If I have opportunities to collaborate with other professionals (e.g. special educators, therapists, paraprofessionals), their expertise and awareness of individual students would make invaluable contributions to appropriate design of assessment measures and interpretation of assessment results.

Tenet 3. Engagement

Key question: How can I stimulate learners' curiosity and emotional connection with the content within a climate of efficacy and belonging?

The effectiveness of my lesson will depend on how well I engage my students' interest from the lesson introduction through the summative assessment. Engagement here means much more than keeping busy; it refers to whether students' brains are actively involved in learning.

Meyer and colleagues (2014) explain that learning will not occur unless students' brain affective networks (i.e., emotional response) are first activated. Students have an emotional response when they are engaged in active reflection about what they already know, anticipate new learning, are hooked by a brief story about someone they can identify with, or see relevance to their own present lives. There is a vast difference in student engagement between a teacher breezing through a summary of prior learning and students being prompted to recall what they already know.

Functional MRI images show increased brain flow to the affective networks of the brain when students are engaged. Teachers laugh when I say, "Too bad you don't have fMRI machines in your classrooms. But you have something just as good—professional observation. You can tell from students' faces whether their brains are engaged or not." Giving students choice in how they will learn and which aspects of knowledge to investigate builds engagement and helps them to develop into more motivated and resilient learners.

In my lesson to provide multiple means of engagement, I would share a video clip, brief story, or news story about a current or historic event that is selected to elicit an emotional response and a sense of relevance in my students. I would ask them to share with a partner or in small groups what they already know about slavery, life of plantation slaves, why slavery wasn't a common practice in the North, and why sometimes brothers faced brothers on the battlefield. I would ask them to generate questions and prompt them to wonder about slavery and the Civil War. I would ask why we would study such a topic today. Their peers' answers would provide more relevance to learning than anything I could say.

I would use two of McREL's instructional strategy categories (2012) during my launching activities and throughout the lesson to maintain engagement. First, in the category Setting Objectives and Providing Feedback, I would ensure that my students were clear about the outcomes of their learning. I would share the knowledge and skill expectations, but I would also ask them to decide which executive skills they personally wanted to target during this lesson. I would assure them that throughout this lesson, as with all my lessons, my intent will be to provide useful guidance and feedback individually to each student progressing as expert learners.

The second McREL instructional strategy category I would use here is Cues, Questions, and Advance Organizers. I would offer sample graphic organizers and coaching on their use to help my students collect pieces of information into an organized visual whole. Ultimately, I would encourage my students to develop their own graphic organizers to increase their independent practice as expert learners.

Finally, engagement also depends upon a sense of belonging. If I am committed to student-centered learning, this lesson would be one more step in my year-long approach to building trusting relationships based on mutual respect and appreciation for individual differences.

Tenet 4. Scaffolded Practice

Key question: How can I offer extra structure for new content being mastered and for individual gaps in background or skills?

As part of my planning, I will need to anticipate whole-group and individual challenges students will face in this lesson and provide scaffolding to support their learning. Scaffolding is a term taken from architecture that describes a temporary structure to hold a worker while constructing, repairing, or cleaning a building. In education, scaffolding refers to a temporary structure used by someone as they learn to perform a task. Young bikers, for example, may use training wheels as they learn to ride. Once they have mastered balance, the training wheels are removed. Of course, some children with certain physical disabilities may always need training wheels, but the ones who don't need them are proud of their independence.

Whole-group scaffolding. Writing a compare-contrast essay based on a variety of references would be a new skill for most of this class. I would use whole-class scaffolding by giving them a guided tour through the steps of preparing their final compare contrast composition. For example, on Monday I would use a simplified topic to model the steps of gathering details for such a project.

To bring humor to our work, I would read the "Three Little Pigs" story and ask them to describe the pigs' perspective of the conflict and reasons why they were right. Using their responses, I would model how to use a two-column organizer. Then I would ask them to imagine the wolf's side of the story and complete the second column with reasons why the wolf was right. After all, in conflicts, don't both sides believe they are right? Can you imagine how much fun they would have?

By the end of the activity, each student would have completed a scaffolded model with ideas organized to write a simple compare contrast essay. On the next day, I would have them use my rubric to analyze the parts of a sample comparative essay and a PowerPoint presentation I wrote from their organizers comparing the pigs' and wolf's perspectives on the conflict. In the process, they would experience using a template for writing their own comparisons.

Individual scaffolding. To determine which students need individual scaffolding, I will draw on data from our school universal screening, MTSS progress monitoring, perspectives of other collaborating professionals, and my own collected observations of how my students perform. For example, Kian has never studied U.S. geography and doesn't know what North and

South mean. Lexi has difficulty getting started. Drew has amazing writing skills, but has little patience for working with peers. Gina has trouble discriminating important from unimportant details in text. Kenzel needs auditory versions of text while he is developing his literacy skills in Tier III sessions.

Because I want each student to choose scaffolding that is exactly what he or she needs, I will offer options for UDL's multiple means of representation. I will provide choices of print and electronic sources that allow my students to customize displays for their perceptual differences and use alternatives for visual and auditory information. Today's technology enables students to clarify or translate vocabulary and symbols, tap into background knowledge, and use highlighting, commenting, and note-taking features. All these examples of scaffolding could be richer if I have other professionals in my classroom to provide extra supports to our students.

As students develop metacognitive skills, they take more ownership of selecting options that work best for them. As active participants in their own learning process, it's more likely that the recognition networks in their brains will recognize and make meaning of new information. Since brain research has confirmed that more learning occurs within social interaction, I would incorporate peer interaction into those scaffolded activities as much as possible.

Tenet 5. Learning Opportunities

Key question: How can my students practice and use the content to develop neural connections of understanding?

Teachers and students who have become accustomed to teacher-centered instruction may feel uncomfortable in this new learning milieu. Rather than teachers painting a picture of clearly organized content for students to digest, students are being invited to make sense of an assortment of seemingly random information. In the process of taming the beast, students develop critical skills needed for lifelong learning and problem solving.

A teacher who is committed to fostering student-centered learning will convey a belief in her students' capacity to lead their own learning. The foundation of trust will not develop overnight and teachers who have been accustomed to teacher-centered instruction may be hesitant to give up control. In early stages of student-centered learning, a teacher may need to provide more scaffolding to grant temporary security for himself and his students.

Eventually, as students develop into independent learners, the teacher can be less directive and move into a facilitator role. Based on formative assessment data she collects, she mentors her students as they follow the plan jointly conceived to develop their skills as expert learners. Bray and McClaskey (2014) state that the teenage passivity that teachers complain about is reduced when students can use choice and voice in planning their own learning in a personalized learning model.

Within my lesson plan, I and any collaborating educators would provide multiple means of action and expression to help students become strategic, goal-directed learners. I would guide them to use their strategic brain networks to plan, organize, and initiate their active interaction with multimedia content. According to Meyer and colleagues (2014), within these learning activities my students would develop executive skills, such as goal setting, strategy development, and their capacity to monitor their own progress.

In my role as facilitator, I would use four of McREL's instructional strategy categories. Students will assume guided ownership with Summarizing and Note taking, Providing Practice, and Identifying Similarities and Differences. Throughout my individual coaching sessions with students, I would implement Reinforcing Effort and Providing Recognition. Underscoring the frequent feedback I provide will be my message that I trust and accept each one as a unique learner with capabilities and potential.

The journey from teacher-centered to student-centered instruction is not an easy one, but the rewards for both teachers and students are worth it as students take more ownership of their learning. Teachers who have been experiencing burnout begin to be revitalized by the student enthusiasm for learning in their classrooms. As with all change, progress is made in small attainable steps, providing that both students and teachers have support to make the transition.

Traditional teacher-centered models of instruction that expect teachers to individualize and differentiate to meet the needs of their students, set unrealistic expectations on teachers' time and available resources. Instead, I propose that teachers can design student-centered lessons using an integrated, five tenet system to support diverse students' mastery of rigorous standards and 21st-century outcomes.

My integrated system incorporates recommendations from the McREL What Works Clearinghouse, Response to Intervention, Universal Design for Learning, and personalized learning. The integrated tenets—learning expectations, assessment, engagement, scaffolded practice, and learning opportunities—are intended to be a framework that teachers and teacher teams can use to plan their approach to student-centered learning.

CHAPTER EIGHT

MANAGING CLASSROOM DYNAMICS

I've learned that people will forget what you said, people will forget what you did, but people will never forget how you made them feel.
MAYA ANGELOU

Sometimes a principal asks me to work with teachers who have weak classroom management. She is hoping that I'll be able to observe them teach once and come up with a few suggestions that will cure the problem. It's not so easy. Teachers who have effective classroom management have taken time to braid together four different skill strands into one seamless system that is uniquely theirs. In Figure 8.1 these strands are illustrated and include interpersonal dynamics at four levels: schoolwide, classroom based, peer to peer, and individual mentoring.

Figure 8.1

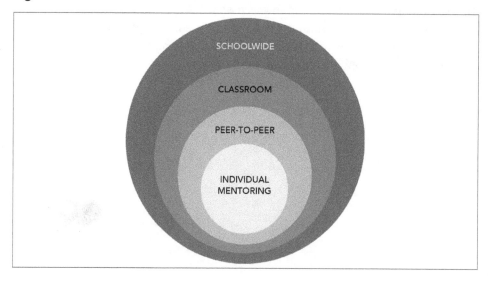

Often the first place to start is with shifting their behavioral system from reactive (i.e., after problem behaviors occur) to proactive (i.e., promoting positive behaviors). Charles (2002) describes the problems with our historic disciplinary approach to classroom management as follows:

> Many of the discipline approaches we have relied on are ineffective, especially those that involve demanding, bossing, scolding, warning, belittling, and punishing. Those tactics can keep behavior partially under control for a while, but they do not last long. Worse, they produce detrimental side effects that inhibit learning, such as uneasiness, fearfulness, evasiveness, avoidance, dishonesty, undesirable attitudes towards learning, overall dislike for school and teachers, inclination to retaliate, and, for many, the desire to leave school as soon as possible. Discipline that produces those results cannot be called effective. Truly effective discipline helps students behave appropriately while maintaining good relations and willingness to cooperate.

If teachers are using disciplinary approaches such as these, I know that any suggestions I make will be greeted with comments, such as "You haven't worked with students like mine," "These students don't care about education," "These kids won't listen to me," or "These kids are lazy." I know that they have decided, perhaps unconsciously, that the situation is outside their control. They have judgments about some or all of their students, and they blame their lack of success on them. There may be plenty of evidence that these students don't fit their profile of committed learners, but these are the students who showed up. Before teachers can design and implement a system, they have to recognize that they have given up and reclaim their power to alter the situation.

Implementing Schoolwide Dynamics

The first strand of classroom management is teachers' ability to incorporate their schoolwide approach to interpersonal dynamics as the foundation for their classroom practice. We would look for core values in the school vision statement, strategic plan, and daily practices. How do adults and youth interact in the school? How are students who are labeled as "different" treated? What behaviors are tolerated or reinforced?

A growing number of schools that are committed to establishing a safe climate conducive to learning use a proactive approach to promoting desired behaviors across the school. Some of these schools focus on acceptance of diversity. Many establish anti-bullying programs. Their efforts increase student and faculty awareness of language and behaviors that exclude others and encourage behaviors that promote inclusion.

The Connect with Kids Network (2016) made the following powerful distinction between tolerance, acceptance, and understanding. They stated that tolerance of those who "differ from us...implies co-existence without meaningful interaction." Acceptance adds that we "come to terms with the fact that the 'others' are not going away, so just deal with the fact that they are here." In contrast, "understanding offers enormous opportunities to learn, grow, and experience the changing world, benefiting us culturally, economically, and personally."

Positive Behavioral Interventions and Supports

The federally funded National Technical Assistance Center on Positive Behavioral Interventions and Supports (PBIS) is a rich resource for schools. Their website contains guidelines for establishing a systemic approach to promote positive behaviors across a whole school. They explain their "emphasis on school-wide systems of support that include proactive strategies for defining, teaching, and supporting appropriate student behaviors to create positive school environments." The PBIS website describes the following four elements that support social competence and academic achievement that focus on staff behavior, student behavior, and shared decision making:

- **Outcomes:** Academic and behavior targets that are endorsed and emphasized by students, families, and educators.

- **Practices:** Evidence-based interventions and strategies to support targeted outcomes.

- **Data:** Information used to identify students' behavioral status, need for change, and effectiveness of practices.

- **Systems:** Supports that are needed to enable the accurate and durable implementation of the practices of PBIS.

BEHAVIOR TARGETS. Generally, PBIS schools identify three behavioral targets such as Respectful, Responsible, and Ready to Learn, and develop clear expectations for these behaviors that students would display in classrooms and other settings (e.g., hallways, cafeteria, buses, and restrooms). Teachers explicitly teach those behaviors and routines.

School faculty members also agree on behavioral offenses that would lead to a discipline office referral or be managed in the classroom. In many cases, a behavior offense would be treated as an opportunity to reteach an expected behavior. For example, a trusted adult would prompt the student to identify which behavior(s) he violated, what he should have done instead, and what he will do now to correct the problem.

PRIMARY PREVENTION. As with Universal Design for Learning (UDL), PBIS has three levels. The intent of the primary level is a universal system to prevent unwanted behaviors and reinforce desirable ones across all school settings. The implementation of the primary level of PBIS greatly reduces the number of students with office referrals who can now remain in the classroom for learning activities.

SECONDARY PREVENTION. The secondary level provides intensive and targeted support to groups of students whose behavior results in disciplinary referrals. Generally, students are counseled to recognize that they need to change some of their behaviors and are willing participants in using group supports to help them make those changes.

TERTIARY PREVENTION. The tertiary prevention level was designed to focus on the needs of individuals who exhibited patterns of problem behavior. The PBIS website (2016) notes that "research has demonstrated the effectiveness of PBIS in addressing the challenges of behaviors that are dangerous, highly disruptive, and/or impede learning and result in social or educational exclusion." The intent is to implement an individualized plan that is cocreated with the student to "diminish problem behavior and, also, to increase the student's adaptive skills and opportunities for an enhanced quality of life."

FUNCTIONAL BEHAVIORAL ANALYSIS (FBA). When a student's behavior warrants the tertiary level, the school assembles a behavior support team to conduct an FBA and develop an individually tailored support plan. This team includes family members, teachers, and behavior specialists who know the student well. They work closely with the student to identify the specific observable problem behavior, the frequency of the behavior, the circumstances (i.e., the antecedents) that seem to trigger the behavior, the purpose of the behavior (i.e., function), such as avoidance or access, the consequences (i.e., positive or negative) currently in place, and possible replacement behaviors.

When I lead FBA meetings, I usually begin by reassuring the student that we all have unhelpful behaviors that we know we should change. When adults admit that changing bad habits is not easy for any of us, the student is more likely to collaborate in planning supports that he needs to alter his behavior patterns. IDEA specifies that a FBA meeting must be conducted for students with disabilities who have serious or frequent behavioral office referrals, whether the school uses PBIS or not. A number of schools find benefits for the youth and the learning environment when they conduct a FBA meeting and implement a support plan sooner than required.

Holcomb (2016) featured a middle school near me for cutting their discipline referrals using PBIS. In just one year, they dropped from over 1,200 students referred to the office to under 30—a 98% reduction. Using all three tiers, they implemented school-wide expectations and taught positive behaviors, employed peer mediators, established a behavior reward system, matched students with adult mentors, and used student input on behavior contracts. All staff distributed reward tickets to students displaying school spirit behaviors in any setting, including cafeterias, hallways, buses, and classrooms. In addition, teachers learned strategies to help students work through minor incidents. This school worked systematically to build a positive learning culture across the whole school and it paid off for them.

Managing Classroom Dynamics

Teachers in schools that have embraced PBIS programs will use the schoolwide behavioral expectations as the foundation of managing classroom dynamics. In schools that have not yet embraced PBIS, teachers can still implement a positive behavior approach in their classrooms. The second strand includes the "way we do things here" kinds of procedures that are specific to the activities in this classroom, including specified routines and acceptable ways of interacting. If other teachers collaboratively teach with them, I encourage joint discussion to agree on these procedures.

Social science research has implications for promoting positive behaviors in the classroom. Miller, Brickman, and Bolen (2012) found that adults can modify children's behaviors more with attribution strategies than persuasion. Persuasion includes providing logical reasons to persuade someone that they should behave in a certain way. For example, a teacher can influence her students' actions by saying, "It's important to throw away your trash as a way to care for our environment." In contrast, a teacher who uses attribution will acknowledge someone for positive attributes they already have as a way to reinforce that behavior. For example, a teacher might say, "I'm pleased that this class does such a good job of picking up after yourselves. You are good stewards of our environment."

They found that by the end of their two-week experiment aimed at decreasing littering both the persuasion and attribution groups improved as compared to a control group, with the attribution group significantly better. However, when they assessed the behavior two weeks later, the attribution group continued to improve, but the persuasion group had fallen off to their pre-test behavior level. In other words, persuasion may make a short-term improvement, but attribution is more likely to improve and sustain behavior change. Which method would be more productive in your classroom?

Establishing Classroom Routines

At the start of the year, most teachers establish routines that create a sense of predictability in their classroom, such as the following:

- Posting essential questions or objectives for student reference to realign on intended lesson outcomes

- Creating a homework submission procedure for how, where, and when work is submitted

- Dedicating a space for supplies and materials and establishing routines for appropriate times to access their lockers and accessing or distributing classroom materials

- Developing an absentee folder or notebook that includes procedures for discovering and accessing missed work

- Using a word wall for illustrated vocabulary that is key to understanding the main concepts of the current unit, posted in a prominent classroom location

- Establishing transition procedures for how students move between different chunks of instruction, change seats, move desks, access materials, and return

- Implement dismissal procedures that allow students time at the end of class to gather their materials, note homework, and verify assignments

It's a joy to observe a classroom where teachers have taken time to explicitly teach, reinforce, and practice these routines. Teachers can strategically establish a classroom climate, clear expectations, and structured opportunities to practice relating to others that will foster social skill development. Teachers who arrange their classrooms in rows and implement only teacher-centered instruction are restricting student growth in this critical area. There is much less down time and less stress when students respond to code words clearly understood by everyone. In addition, these predictable routines are essential for students with disabilities to succeed.

Establishing Fair Is Not Equal

Teachers sometimes worry that students will complain about unfair treatment if a few students get extra scaffolding or accommodations. I respond that nobody complains that some students need glasses and invite them to use that example in response.

Two teachers recently shared with me their proactive approach to fairness. One makes a startling announcement to her class at the beginning of the year to spark awareness of how fairness doesn't mean that everyone is treated the same. With a smile, she shares that one student needs a daily insulin shot. She told the nurse that wasn't fair because others would feel left out. So starting tomorrow all students will get a shot. Believe me, she got her students' attention. They were glad to be treated unequally.

Another teacher shows a cartoon of five animals—a monkey, a fish, a dog, an elephant, and a bird—that lined up to take a test. All would have to climb the tree to pass the test. Was that fair? Both teachers used their students' outraged responses to spark a discussion. They assured their classes that to be fair each student would get what he needed—even if it wasn't equal. By initiating these discussions at the beginning of the year, teachers establish ground rules for individualizing instruction and give students permission to seek the supports that each student needs.

Incorporating Engagement Research

One of the best ways to maintain positive behaviors in the classroom is to use approaches that are engaging for students. The Marzano Research Laboratory has built a reputation for translating large-scale research into specific classroom applications. Their publication on classroom engagement practices asserts that with these practices "every teacher can create a classroom environment in which engagement is the norm instead of the exception." Henley (2006) notes that when students are engaged, their behavior is more likely to be appropriate in a learning environment, reducing behavioral disruptions. The Marzano and Pickering (2011) model for engagement is based on the following four components:

- **Emotions:** Encouraging positive feelings (such as enthusiasm, enjoyment, and zest rather than boredom, anxiety, or shame) and high energy that is largely influenced by feeling accepted and a teacher's positive demeanor.

- **Interest:** Sparking students' interest over time with game-like activities, friendly controversy, unusual information, and effective questioning strategies.

- **Perceived importance:** Building on students' personal sense of self and life goals with challenging real-life contexts for problem solving.

- **Perceptions of efficacy:** Fostering students' creation of future possible selves who are capable and accomplished.

Infusing Brain Research

Dieker (2007) summarized differences between adolescent male and female brains. Males are more likely to need experiential and kinesthetic learning with opportunities to manipulate objects. When faced with lots of words in lessons, their hormone responses lead to more impulsivity and reduced attention. On the other hand, females thrive on interaction, especially if it involves sharing feelings and empathy. They prefer verbally based lessons and need fewer brain breaks than males. Teachers who are aware of these gender differences will provide opportunities that appeal to both males and females.

Brain research provides teachers a basis for three other classroom practices that are effective with adolescents—repetition, movement, and laughter (Dieker, 2007). First, adolescents, especially those with disabilities, need frequent repetition to move information from short-term memory into long-term memory. Teachers can expose students to key concepts in multiple ways and incorporate reviews into their lessons, especially using graphic organizers.

Second, teachers who build movement into their lesson will discover that activity stimulates concentration and provides valuable brain breaks in the midst of complex learning. The movement can be as simple as saying, "Stand up if you agree with the statement that…," "Pat your head to help you think," or "Walk to your two o'clock partner to share one idea from today's lesson."

I don't know who started clock partners but I'm delighted with all the creative ways teachers use them. At the beginning of the year or marking period, students invite 12 peers to be their clock partners. For example, Sean and Renata agree to be six o'clock partners and write each other's names at the six on their clock faces. Some teachers tell them to leave the 12 o'clock slot blank so they can match two students—sometimes one with stronger reading skills with another who has weaker reading skills. Once students have practiced the routine for finding their partners and returning to their seats, teachers can use clock partners to give students an organized way to reinforce their learning with a variety of partners. They also discover that movement gives students renewed energy to focus on the lesson.

Third, Dieker (2007) advocates laughter. She says, "Laughter is not only helpful for mastering academic content, but is also a great way to relieve stress." She suggests ways to include humor in the classroom, such as making up a funny story to remember key content facts, teachers poking fun at themselves (and modeling how to laugh at yourself), having a two-minute laughing contest to see who has the funniest laugh, and using funny cartoons to illustrate lessons. In an inclusive classroom, it would be important to distinguish between laughing with others and laughing at others.

Encouraging Peer Dynamics

The third strand of interactions that effective teachers include in their personal system is approaches that encourage positive peer interactions and effective peer supported learning. An inclusive environment is the perfect place for all students to learn how to relate to diverse individuals in future adult environments. Wachtel (2011) created a list of the top 13 reasons for being fired and nearly half of these reasons were related to interpersonal issues in the workplace.

Setting the Stage for Interpersonal Mores

Teachers have more power than they realize in establishing a learning environment where all students experience the safety and acceptance they need to flourish. My favorite quotation by Goethe sums up their influence:

> I have come to the frightening conclusion that I am the decisive element. It is my personal approach that creates the climate. It is my daily mood that makes the weather. I possess tremendous power to make a life miserable or joyous. I can be a tool of torture or an instrument of inspiration. I can humiliate or humor, hurt or heal. In all situations, it is my response that decides whether a crisis is escalated or de-escalated, and a person humanized or dehumanized.

This sentiment applies to more than how teachers treat their students. If they notice students exhibiting behavior that creates "us versus them" polarization or diminishes anyone's value in their classroom, the teacher needs to address it immediately. By saying nothing, teachers condone such behavior. In October 2014, the U.S. Department of Education, Office for Civil Rights issued a letter urging schools to respond to "an ever-increasing number of complaints concerning the bullying of students with disabilities and the effects of that bullying on their education, including on the special education and related services to which they are entitled."

Teachers who promote positive peer interactions can prevent many of these instances of bullying and harassment. But building positive peer relations goes beyond preventing bullying. The social need to belong is strong in adolescents as in all human cultures. Baumeister and Tice (2012) summarized a series of experiments with college students that investigated the effects of rejection and social isolation. They found the following responses:

- **Numbness:** Decreased sensitivity to physical pain and emotional feeling

- **Hostility and aggression:** Verbal and behavioral actions toward others, not just the ones who had excluded them
- **Reduced prosocial behavior:** Less likely to initiate positive social interactions or to feel empathy for someone else's experience
- **Decreased intelligence:** Sharp drop in intelligent thought and logical reasoning
- **Loss of self control:** More likely to participate in self-destructive indulgences
- **Less attention regulation:** Difficulty with focus and attention
- **Distrustful of others:** Preferring to avoid another rejection

Harrist & Bradley (2002) offer the following interventions to address social isolation and rejection, whether the student is disliked, ignored, or hangs on the periphery of the peer group.

- **Change the unaccepted youth** by "teaching more socially appropriate behaviors" or "focusing on underlying social-cognitive process thought to drive the problem behavior."
- **Use a peer mediator approach** by reducing peer rejection or isolation with a selected peer who acts as a model or reinforcer of appropriate behavior.
- **Address peer group exclusion** by developing empathy and understanding using approaches such as social stories, reflective discussions, and promoting classroom practices that support students to internalize and generalize inclusive behaviors.

Incorporating Cooperative Learning

Engaging learning environments will provide frequent opportunities for positive peer interactions. Teenagers love such activities, but teachers frequently tell me that group work doesn't work. They're right. If they simply put students in groups to complete a task without any structure, it won't work. One student frequently does most of the work and at least one student hitchhikes. Without structure, it is unlikely that all students will learn or that they will expand their skills at getting along. But structured collaborative-cooperative learning is powerful.

Panitz (1999) clarified the difference between collaborative and cooperative learning. "Collaboration is a philosophy of interaction and personal lifestyle where individuals are responsible for their actions, including learning and respecting the abilities and contributions of their peers. Cooperation is a structure of interaction designed to facilitate the accomplishment of a specific end product or goal through people working together in groups."

In other words, collaborative learning is more process-centered while cooperative learning is more product-centered. I think the line between the two is blurry, and I'm not sure that it makes much difference. In both cases, students learn more by working together. Most classrooms today will want to implement structures so that students practice both collaborative and cooperative learning skills.

Here are some popular cooperative learning activities from Dieker (2007) and Hollas (2007):

- **Jigsaw:** Each student becomes an expert on a specific content and teaches others in his group.

- **Four corners:** Students are invited to select one of four answers to a question and join others in a corner to discuss reasons to support their response.

- **Numbered heads together:** Each student in a group is assigned a number and work together to solve a question or problem. When the teacher calls a number, that person responds for the group.

- **Role cards:** Each student has a laminated role card that explains his or her role in the group for expository text (e.g., key word finder, main idea minder, detail person, or question asker), narrative text (e.g., predictor, summarizer, clarifier, or questioner), or brainstorming (e.g., manager, coach, reporter, or talent scout). I especially like this last one that uses sports-related roles. The job of the talent scout is to go steal ideas from other teams.

All these activities and others can be more effective with building a learning culture in the classroom if they are structured according to the following seven principles adapted from Kagan (2013):

- Establish routine signals so students know when to begin and end cooperative groups

- Ensure individual accountability with clear expectations for each student's contribution

- Clarify group accountability with specific expectations for targeted learning and products

- Build positive interdependence with all students valued for their contributions

- Plan for equal participation so that students do not do more or less than their share

- Provide scaffolding for students as needed

- Include opportunities for reflective evaluation of each member's contributions including themselves

Using Kagan Cooperative Learning Structures

Two years ago, I was delighted to learn about the work of Spencer Kagan who has published his research since 1968. Kagan Structures are designed to engage every student. The bold claim in the preface to his introductory mini book is "...structures improve academic achievement, reduce the achievement gap, develop thinking skills, reduce discipline problems, improve race relations, foster character development, and increase social skills, self-esteem, and liking for class and content" (Kagan, 2013). I discovered those benefits when I introduced Kagan structures in my workshops and started using them with teachers.

The Kagan website offers a range of resources that describe how to use their structures in specific content areas. The site suggests that teachers begin with five powerful structures that can be adapted for any content. My favorite is called Round Robin.

Imagine that I want my students to discuss character motivation after reading *Tom Sawyer*. My student desks are in groups of four, with each student assigned one of the characters: Tom, Huck, Becky, and Aunt Polly. I instruct each student to write one question about motivation he would like to ask the other three characters. Then I ask the number two student in each group to stand and introduce her character to the group, "Hello there, I'm

Aunt Polly." Going clockwise around the group, each person asks Aunt Polly a question such as "Why did you make Tom whitewash the fence?"

In the process, students explore character motivation, but they also practice listening skills using the routine I've taught them. The person asking the question will summarize as follows "So, you think it's your parenting job to make sure Tom learns responsibility?" As students work around the group, the members prompt the character standing if he doesn't recall the event in question. The students are clear that the purpose is to review the events of the plot and explore character motivation, but there is also the purpose of reinforcing each member's participation. Before each character sits down, the group responds with a positive gambit, such as "Thank you, Aunt Polly, for sharing." Each group member compliments her for something specific about her responses.

Each Kagan Structure builds positive interdependence, individual accountability, equal participation, and simultaneous interaction. More importantly, these structures build cooperation, not competition in the classroom. Students learn to give each other immediate reinforcement. This activity is collaborative in nature.

This activity would move from being collaborative to cooperative if it was used as a precursor to a writing composing assignment. Students could use details that were discussed in their Kagan Round Robin group as a basis for this prompt: Select any character in Tom Sawyer and write the two or three top values that guided his or her actions. Provide details from the novel to illustrate the values you selected. After our Round Robin, no student would be able to say, "I have nothing to write."

Exploring Individual Dynamics

At the heart of it, teachers develop their own styles of relating to each student individually. Special educators, paraeducators, and related service providers who spend limited time in general education classrooms may have little influence on the first three interpersonal dynamics strands. Their impact on interpersonal dynamics will center on personal relationships.

When I was at Towson University, I repeatedly witnessed the significance of one-on-one personal relationships. When I interviewed prospective graduate students, I always asked, "Why do you want to become a special educator?" Every candidate responded with a story about a person who had profoundly impacted his life. They spoke about siblings, fellow classmates, students they had tutored or mentored, or children in summer camp. Their eyes glowed in a far-off way as they recalled how it felt to make a difference with someone who was courageous, invincible, funny, or fragile. I believe that most educational professionals decided to enter the field either because of such experiences or because a teacher had made a difference in their lives.

At the bottom line, all teaching comes down to building individual relationships with our students. We can all think of past teachers who encouraged us and believed in us as individuals. We worked our fingers off for those teachers. My 4th-grade teacher, Mrs. Fertell, told me that I was a gifted writer. I wrote her a 23-page book report on *The Black Stallion*. My parents let me stay up all night to finish it. On the other hand, all of us remember at least one teacher who didn't like us or treated us unfairly. Whether those impressions were true or not, I know that I didn't work as hard for them.

A presenter at a conference shared a study that I haven't forgotten (although I haven't been able to find it in print). He described a high school that wanted to institute a new dropout prevention practice. They learned that students who are not connected to at least one adult are more likely to drop out. The principal at this school invited all faculty and staff to a meeting. Pointing to the roster of students taped up around the room, the principal asked each person to mark with a check the students they could greet by name in the hall and star any students if they knew something personal about the student's life outside of school.

When everyone had finished, about 10% of the students had no marks by their names. The administration set up mentoring relationships for those students with teachers, guidance, cafeteria staff, or custodial staff. I recall that their initiative greatly reduced the dropout statistics, but more importantly, they reinforced the importance of ensuring that each student belongs.

Building Relationships

The impact of teachers' relationships with individual students can't be overstated. Rosenthal (2002) described the famous 1965 Pygmalion Experiment in which elementary teachers across a whole school were told the results of intelligence testing, indicating that 20% of their students (chosen at random) would show surprising intellectual gains over the course of the school year. End-of-the-year retesting revealed that those identified children did indeed show greater intellectual gain than did the children of the control group.

Bonding with students comes naturally for some teachers, but others may need guidelines. Cummings (2000) makes the following recommendations for teachers committed to building relationships with students:

- **Make one-on-one relationships:** Greet each student daily as he or she enters the room, learn each name as soon as possible, and make time to interact and become acquainted with each one individually.

- **Use appropriate self-disclosure:** Reveal personal experiences and feelings that are helpful to students while maintaining professional distance.

- **Network to build a community:** Connect with families and build a classroom network.

- **Establish traditions:** Use routines like regular journaling, newsletters, and homework that involves families and peers.

As each teacher develops her own style, she will want to consider the key values she wants to embody in her relationships with students. Will students learn self-reliance or kindness? Teamwork or striving for ambitious goals? Risk taking or appreciation? Teachers don't need to agree on their key values. One of the benefits of having multiple teachers is that students will grow in different ways under the influence of different teachers. What is important is that teachers have reflected on the values they will embody in their classrooms and reinforce a small number of them.

One way to build a positive, empowering relationship with each youth is Markova and McArthur's approach in *I Am Smart* (2015). They point out how much attention is focused on what students can't do in school. For example, Javier will get his spelling test back with his 16 misspelled words marked wrong. What if, instead, the teacher prompted him to consider the approach he used to get the other four words right?

They recommend focusing on how Javier is smart rather than on how smart Javier is. If you have ever watched a toddler learning to walk, you will see that there is no one right way to learn, but instead, each child figures it out for himself. In the same way, each individual has unique ways of grappling with making meaning of new information.

Markova and McArthur (2015) recommend that parents create a positive passport for each child based on the belief that their "child has the innate ability to solve challenges and can use questions to help them figure out what they need." Teachers could do the same thing. Their work is based on the following four principles:

- **Differences are resources, not disorders:** Accepting that diverse perspectives and unique approaches to situations expand, not limit, what is possible.

- **Track assets, not deficits:** Helping youth to compile a list of strengths and supporting them to use those assets when they get stuck.

- **See mistakes as experiments, not failures:** Coaching students to learn from experiments, including reflecting on why some tasks feel harder or insurmountable.

- **Learn from the inside out as well as the outside in:** Teaching students to reflect on their own metacognitive processes and overcome the challenges they face.

As schools move from teacher-centered learning into student-centered learning, teachers will move from instructor into the role of mentor. Randolph and Johnson (2008) define mentoring as a "relationship between an older, more experienced adult and an unrelated, younger protégé—a relationship in which the adult provides ongoing guidance, instruction, and encouragement aimed at developing the competence and character of the protégé."

Mentoring will provide more opportunities for individual coaching to empower youth to become reflective and resilient lifelong learners. In the end, these students prosper from the attention of caring adults, and those adults become re-energized by the professional satisfaction of making a difference in young lives.

New Possibilities for Accountability

The 2015 ESSA guidelines introduced new possibilities for school accountability. While we await the final regulations, I have been reviewing speculative blogs from reputable sources. Blad (2016) summarizes the provision as follows in a recent *Education Week* article:

A portion of the *Every Student Succeeds Act* that requires states to incorporate nonacademic factors into their accountability systems could help promote a broader vision of school success that extends beyond traditional measures, such as standardized-test scores, educators and policy watchers say. ... Specifically, the new law requires states to use at least one "indicator of school quality or student success" that "allows for meaningful differentiation in school performance" and "is valid, reliable, comparable, and statewide," alongside academic data in their accountability systems. Schools must also be able to disaggregate data related to that indicator to show how it affects students in different subpopulations: those from all racial and ethnic groups, students with disabilities, children from low-income families, and English-language learners.

The author expresses the general agreement that the new indicator selected by states will become a focus of scrutiny by educators, families, and school boards. More than that, it will become a target area for improving professional competence. He speculates about measuring students' engagement, social-emotional skills (such as grit), and safe school climate. These articles caution that it will take time to develop valid measures of these nonacademic markers of student growth.

Teachers are faced with the challenge of establishing a classroom learning climate based on acceptance of diverse learners and development of interpersonal skills. Effective teachers develop their own personal style weaving together the following four strands— schoolwide expectations for learning, including PBIS; classroom-based routines, mores, and practices; peer-to-peer collaborative and cooperative learning activities; and individual relationship building that reinforce a teacher's key values.

CHAPTER NINE

YOUTH EMPOWERMENT

Success is achieved by developing our strengths, not by eliminating our weaknesses.

MARILYN VOS SAVANT

The ultimate point of this book is to support youth as they develop into productive adults. If we examine current statistics, it becomes clear that this is a serious problem. Stark and Noel (2015) reported that the dropout rate in this country in 2012 was three times higher for students with disabilities than those without. Dropouts earn significantly less income over the course of their lives and are more likely to be on the public dole through welfare or penal systems. Stoddard (2014) reported census data from 2014 that showed that 34% of adults with disabilities were employed as compared with 74% of adults without disabilities. Clearly, our current practices aren't working.

Based on my years of experience in classrooms, I think the issue centers on whether students are empowered as causal agents in their own life. When I walk into classrooms where students have their heads down, I can predict the scenario. Teachers will give assignments, and students will ignore them or passively comply. Students will perform minimally on projects and tests, and teachers will lower their expectations. Ultimately, teachers will blame the students for their apathy, and students blame the teachers for being boring.

When this passive, nonlearning culture has persisted in one classroom or across the whole school, it becomes a toxic environment for teachers and students alike. Fortunately, there has been an explosion of exciting school reform initiatives reversing these patterns. Many of these initiatives fall under the umbrella of personalized learning in which teachers have flexibility to design creative ways to engage students as designers of their own learning tasks. When students have voice and choice for their own learning tasks and have guidance and individualized feedback on their progress from adults who care, they become active learners.

Students with disabilities are more likely to succeed academically and socially in inclusive personalized learning environments since the learning activities and assessment measures can be tailored to their individual profiles. As shown in Figure 9.1, students with disabilities will need additional mentoring in four dimensions to become empowered as lifelong self-advocates.

Figure 9.1

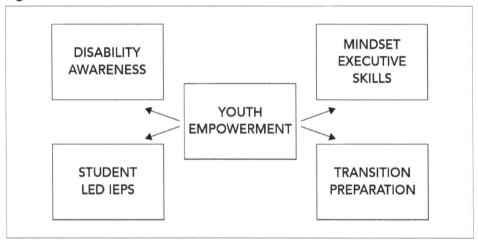

Increasing Disability Awareness

Students with disabilities will only have access to accommodations following graduation if they self disclose; therefore, it's important that they know as much as possible about their own disability. They should be able to explain their diagnosis, the terms associated with it, and how their disability impacts their ability to perform and achieve. They also need to know which accommodations and supports work for them in various types of situations so that they can self-advocate.

If professionals and families have never discussed details of their disability with these students by the time they have become teenagers, each one has probably already constructed a story to explain why they are different from everyone else. Those stories aren't pretty. They include self-descriptions like stupid, weird, klutzy, loner, nerd, and loser.

In the late 1980s our local vocational rehabilitation (VR) office had a grant to pilot disability awareness classes for teenagers with learning disabilities. As a district transition coordinator, I arranged for the VR counselor to visit two high schools for five 45-minute sessions.

During the first session, she introduced the project by telling students they were chosen because they had learning disabilities (LD). She was not prepared for their angry responses. They shouted that they did not have disabilities. They crossed their arms and wouldn't look at her. They refused to be part of the group. She did her best to reassure them and then she cut the meeting short. The teachers and I pleaded with them to give her another chance, but it wasn't easy. When we bribed them, offering a pizza party following the fifth session, they reluctantly agreed.

During the second and third meetings, she pointedly conveyed respect and admiration. She told them that their futures weren't limited, but it was important for them to understand and cope with their specific LD. She drew diagrams on the board about brain function and described different types of LD. She emphasized that LD did not mean stupid. She reminded them of famous people with LD and elicited creative strategies they already used every day to compensate for learning problems. Students asked when she would be back.

By the fifth session, these students were advocating for themselves in class. They explained to their teachers and classmates that they learned differently. They started being strategic in their approach to school assignments. Their shame at having a disability seemed to have evaporated. But where did that shame come from?

I recall discussions at Breakthrough Disability institutes about the culture of crippleness. Art Nierenberg helped us to see that we grow up in a tradition of prejudice against those with handicaps, disabilities, disfigurement, and antisocial behaviors. Everyone has heard historic accounts of deformed babies abandoned in sacrifice, shunned leper colonies, freak shows, and sterilization of defective persons.

Until recently, Hollywood characters with disabilities were typically subjects of scorn or ridicule. Most children labeled uneducable in this country were not included in public schools until 1975. When Art went to the mall, parents told their children not to stare or talk to that man in a wheelchair. Did they think his polio left him contagious? This invisible yet pervasive culture is insidious. It carries low expectations, disrespect, and hopelessness for the individual and the people connected with them. The worst part is that the culture of crippleness has affected us all, and we don't even see it.

The students in this project had been deeply influenced by this culture. Afterwards, they shared the following reactions to learning the specifics of their learning disability:

- "I thought something must be really wrong with me since it was such a big secret."
- "I became the class clown so I could pretend I didn't mind when kids laughed at me."
- "I figured it was better to be the bad kid than the dumb kid."
- "How come nobody told me this stuff before? Now I can do something about it!"

In the days when I was a special education teacher, I adjusted my teaching for each student's individual needs, but it never occurred to me to let them know what I was doing. I also never thought to ask for their opinions about which strategies worked better for them.

If I were in a classroom today, I would have individual conferences with each student, opening their confidential folder to share with them. I would make sure they understood the relevant terms so that they could talk intelligently about themselves. More importantly, I would have ongoing conversations with them about learning strategies, mindset research, and executive function. As we learned from our project, students need more than a one-time conversation to grasp the implications of their disabilities for their future dreams. Ultimately, I would expose the culture of crippleness for what it is—a fictitious sentence of hopelessness. Self-knowledge gives them choice for their future and puts them in the driver's seat.

Incorporating Mindset and Executive Skills

According to Carol Dweck (2006), our approach to learning can be boiled down to two mindsets— a fixed mindset based on the belief that our ability and capacity are fixed at birth and unlikely to change; and a growth mindset based on the belief that putting effort into learning challenging material will help our brains grow.

We all have a fixed mindset about learning certain types of things. For example, people say "I don't have a green thumb" or "I have two left feet" or "I have no artistic ability." We smile and accept their judgment that some people are simply missing certain talents. But when a student says, "I can't write" or "I don't get math just like my father," that's a problem. They are so sure of failure that they won't even try.

Dweck (2006) discovered that people with growth mindset relish difficult tasks. Brain research informs us that activities that stretch our thinking also expand the neurons and increase our thinking capacity. Just like scientists, we learn more from failed attempts when we have a growth mindset.

I work with many teachers who have incorporated discussions of growth mindset into their teaching practice. They teach students that intelligence is malleable, not fixed, and that it will expand through their effort, focus, and diligent practice. They praise students for tackling challenging tasks and persisting when the learning gets tough whether they succeed or not. They found that for some students, understanding the difference between a fixed and growth mindset made a big difference. For those students, the missing piece could simply be their effort and willingness to persist. When those students started putting forth the effort to learn, they discovered that they could be successful.

Following a workshop I conducted on mindset, I became curious about another group of students who didn't respond to mindset-building instructional approaches. Teachers described students who tried to succeed, but their significant knowledge gaps, skill deficits, and habitual behaviors had resulted in failure. Just changing their mindset was not enough. Their perspective on their future was bleak and entrenched. No amount of cheerleading by adults around them changed their hopelessness. Over time, they had accumulated evidence of their own inadequacy from being ridiculed and disciplined, not to mention their own observations that they were less capable than their peers.

Their predicaments are worsened by the impersonal nature of traditional schools that are organized like factories. Teachers dispense knowledge into rows of students who are expected to sit patiently and wait for knowledge deposits. This picture appears exaggerated except to those who have seen other possibilities. Personalized classrooms are based on the assumption that each child is unique and learns in different ways. This humanized approach to fostering learning reduces or eliminates students' humiliation at not learning within traditional, one-size-fits-all systems.

Attribution Theory (Wilson, Damiani, & Shelton, 2002), a term from social psychology, may be useful to teachers as they provide personalized coaching to students who don't seem to respond to strategies that work with other students. All of us explain our problems or successes, attributing the causes to internal factors (i.e., something we did) or external factors (i.e., something outside our control). Teachers who take the time to ask students about their explanations may discover that their explanations are not empowering. For example, if Trey thinks his poor grade is because the teacher doesn't like him, or if Laverne explains her passing score to luck, they will not see that their actions can make a difference in their achievement.

Learned helplessness, when a student's behavior communicates a belief that he can't achieve without help, represents the "debilitating effects of a lack of control over negative outcomes" (Wilson, Damiani, & Shelton, 2002). Teachers can implement reattribution interventions, encouraging students to generate new explanations for their successes or failures that provide them an avenue to improved performance. It takes time, but it is worth it.

One district decided to tackle the issue of these disenfranchised, discouraged students head-on with a focus on executive skills. I conducted an October workshop on identifying executive skills deficits, such as organization, goal-directed persistence, sustained attention, task initiation, planning, prioritizing, time management, and stress tolerance. I shared resources and strategies for remediating those skills, especially encouraging teachers to use student conferencing to identify deep seated self-efficacy issues.

After participating in my workshop, the special education teachers developed their own plan to apply what they learned. Of the 28 teachers participating, eight decided to reinforce executive skills with a whole class.

They worked in partnership with a general education teacher to incorporate specific executive skills into their classroom instruction.

The other 20 special educators each selected one or two students on their caseload and explicitly addressed their individual executive skills weaknesses. All of them intended to work one on one with their case study students to build students' metacognitive awareness of the unique way their own brain functions and habitual behaviors that may be unproductive. They tailored coaching to the individual students according to specific learning tasks where students were already struggling.

When we met again in February, they completed a survey about what they had learned as they applied executive skills to their coaching of students. Of 26 responding teachers, 100% reported improved understanding of executive skills, 85% were better able to examine what could be triggering a student who struggles, and 96% were better able to speak about a student's executive functioning needs in an IEP meeting.

Teachers who build empowering relationships with their students with disabilities will provide them structured opportunities so they can experience success and begin to open the door to possibilities for self-efficacy. Gaskill and Hoy (2002) define self-efficacy as "people's beliefs in their capabilities specific to a particular task." Through their research, they documented the following four sources of personal self-efficacy:

1. **Mastery experiences:** Related to the task

2. **Emotional arousal:** Feeling psyched and excited as opposed to feeling anxious

3. **Vicarious experiences:** Observing mastery modeled by similar peers one identifies with

4. **Verbal persuasion:** Pep talk or specific performance feedback from someone with credibility, trustworthiness, and expertise in the task

Knowing these four sources, teachers can support youth to expand their personal self-efficacy. It isn't enough to have students achieve success with a difficult skill. Each student must take time to self-acknowledge and recognize that she has mastered something she previously thought impossible. We all develop self-efficacy from consciously collecting evidence that we CAN, especially when we have amassed convincing evidence to the contrary.

Preparing for Transition

Special education law requires that we conduct ongoing transition assessments to determine students' career interests, preferences, strengths, and needs. Further, it requires that we tailor their high school activities to prepare them for their declared post-school outcomes. The reauthorization of the *Workforce Innovation and Opportunity Act* of 2014 provides additional resources to support school efforts to prepare in-school and out-of-school at-risk youth to be productive members of the workforce.

Preparing for Careers

I was the resident inclusion coach in a magnet vocational high school that built instruction for all students around preparation for college and careers, both inside and outside the school building. Ninth graders took a career exploration course in which they investigated a range of careers with opportunities to reflect on which of these career pathways appealed to them. Their assignments included visiting workplaces, electronically and during field trips. They also discussed potential employment opportunities and preparation.

On the announced day, students dressed for success to participate in mock job interviews for the job of their choice. This school invited local business representatives to serve as interviewers. When they weren't scheduled for interviews, these men and women visited classes to share in depth about careers in their field and describe a typical day on the job. They answered questions about related postsecondary education and early career experiences available while still in high school.

Students were highly motivated to prepare for that day, and the excitement for their futures lingered long after. What was different about that school was the way they sustained a futures approach. Anytime I visited an academic classroom, I saw evidence that teachers, regardless of the subject, related their curriculum to future careers. Problem solving in the sciences, math, social studies, and English were tied into real-life problems that have been solved or still awaiting new approaches. Career exploration was ongoing and continuous. The dropout rate in that school continues to be one of the lowest in the state.

Transition preparation can be broadened beyond school if students are empowered to do the investigating. When they go with their families to a sporting event, shopping center, recreational facility, or use public transportation, they can speculate about the jobs that are needed to support those resources.

Research indicates that students with paid jobs before they graduate are more likely to be employed after leaving school. What local resources could support your youth to explore careers and empower them to prepare for transition into productive adulthood?

Preparing for College Transition

When I was the state transition specialist, I became acquainted with Linda Schnapp who started Project Access at Howard Community College in Maryland. Their service delivery model was groundbreaking in 1997 and funded with a federal model demonstration grant. I recently visited them and was delighted to learn that 19 years later, they are still going strong.

Project Access offers a four-week summer institute for high school students with disabilities to help them explore college possibilities and develop skills needed for success in college. The institute includes classes to boost academic skills, especially math, study skills, reading, and expository writing. Rather than remediating weak skills, they teach strategies students can use as future college students, including internet research, study skills, and preparing research papers. With guidance, they apply for college admission and financial aid and practice advocating for accommodations.

Throughout the institute, these high school students visit college classes and meet with professors to learn about college expectations. They also take field trips to nearby four-year colleges to expose them to all sides of college experience including classrooms, dining halls, dormitories, game rooms, admissions office, disability support services offices, and meeting other students with disabilities.

Breaking the odds, 85-90% of students who participate in Project Access enroll in college. Many begin at a community college and transfer to four-year universities. Nineteen years of experience proves that students with the right supports can make it in college. What kinds of supports do your students have to transition to college?

Think College is an exciting federally funded center at the University of Massachusetts with a powerful internet presence. Since its inception in 2010, it has provided technical assistance to local colleges and communities across the country to provide college opportunities for youth with intellectual disabilities. Previously, this population and the adults who support them never would have considered college as an option. Think College research findings, gathered from 27 federally funded model demonstration projects across the country, describe the opportunities for 883 students who were able to participate in college courses, internships, and integrated community employment through those programs. I love to share their video documentaries of these students and watch the faces of teachers and families as they begin to consider college as a possibility.

Incorporating Assistive Technology

Assistive technology (AT) in special education law is defined as "any item, piece of equipment, software, or product system that is used to increase, maintain, or improve the functional capabilities of individuals with disabilities." The explosion in technology in recent years has made this an exciting field, but secondary schools often lag behind. Although the law requires that IEP teams evaluate whether students need assistive technology, most schools in my experience only investigate the need for assistive technology for students who have sensory impairments (i.e., vision or hearing impairments) or who have significant communication needs.

I recall being part of a vocational school acceptance committee debate in the early 1980s. Christine, an applicant for the cosmetology program had scored well in her entrance interview and dexterity test. However, she also had severe dyslexia. The committee had never admitted a nonreader before. Their program funding was dependent on the percentage of students who graduated and passed licensing exams. Could a nonreader pass the licensing exam for cosmetology? For Christine, they decided to take a risk. They were relieved when she became a model student. She assumed responsibility for using audio texts for her academics and technical cosmetology science. In her senior year, she was elected president of her class. Because she proved that students with disabilities can succeed, that school expanded their policy for admission of students with disabilities.

Disability service centers on college campuses frequently offer workshops for students with disabilities to introduce them to AT that can make learning easier. But is that too late? Many more students would consider college an option if they already used AT during high school. Schools with one-to-one technology initiatives that give a laptop or tablet to each student are already halfway there. They normalize technology that could have been stigmatizing.

High schools are beginning to encourage students with disabilities to use AT and personal devices to give students more ownership in the following aspects of the learning process:

- **Reading support:** Every computer, laptop, tablet, and phone has settings for accessibility. By changing the settings, any device can read text aloud. There are other software and apps that will also define words you highlight and allow you to write text annotations.

- **Writing support:** Most people are familiar with software and apps that provide word prediction, spell check, and grammar check. Other programs will convert speech into text, help with outlining, tracking bibliography sources, and organizing note cards. Sometimes students use the text-to-speech feature to listen to what they've written.

- **Listening and note taking:** Smartpens are great devices for taking notes while recording classroom lectures or discussion. I could have used one when I was in my doctoral program, but I frequently use one now when I am in strategy meetings so I can listen later to anything I missed in my notes.

- **Study skills:** Software and applications can provide support for studying, creating flashcards, and using graphic organizers.

- **Scheduling and time management:** Calendars and phones make it easy to set alarms and reminders to help students manage their time and tasks.

When using technology becomes normalized at an early age and students are given voice and choice of how, when, and what technological supports they will use, they will broaden their hopes and expectations for successful futures in postsecondary education and careers.

Supporting Student-led IEPs

Some of my best moments as a consultant have been the times when teachers shared outcomes of empowering students to lead all or parts of their IEP meetings. My website includes links to many resources on the internet that teachers can use to prepare students to take a leadership role in their own IEP.

I don't know why student-led IEPs haven't become the norm. Think about the unspoken communication to a teenage boy when a group of adults assemble and deliver their summary of his current functioning. He will probably mainly listen for his failings. Then they propose draft goals they have developed for his improvement. Does this really make sense? How would you feel if a group developed a plan for how you should improve over the next year? Why are we surprised that these youths don't take responsibility for their education or their futures when we haven't given them responsibility for their present? Emmanuel M. D. Jenkins, motivational speaker, has it right when he tells youth in his audience, "Life is like a car. It will take you wherever you want to go, but you have to get in the driver's seat."

I encourage teachers and transition specialists to phase in student-led IEPs because the adults will need time to adjust to letting students lead. Start with just a few students or start with having students share their post-school educational and career goals. As youths are ready, they can assume leadership for more aspects of their IEP meeting.

One high school I worked with started with 9th graders as the master of ceremony at their IEP meeting, using a script to invite professionals' or parents' perspectives on aspects of their plan. Each year, students added more responsibilities such as preparing a slide show presentation with pictures to share their interests, hobbies, career interests, and work-related experiences. They eventually gathered teachers' perspectives of their current level of functioning and used these perspectives as a basis for drafting their own IEP goals.

Teachers are typically hesitant to launch student-led IEPs because they don't know what to expect. Once they have tried it with a few students, they can't wait to do it with them all. They rave about the transformation with their students. They report that students are now open to understanding more about their own learning process and managing their own learning strategies.

Teachers who work as coaching mentors, regardless of their titles, will find ways to empower students to take ownership for their own success and their own lives. They help each student to understand his unique disability and reverse limiting effects of the culture of crippleness and stereotype threat. They use their professional judgment to recognize issues with fixed mindset or executive skills that interfere with their students' progress. They prompt each student to begin to identify specific learning strategies that work best for them in particular situations. They encourage their students to explore transition experiences that will help them clarify post-school goals. Finally, they coach students to take leadership roles in their IEP meeting.

All of these activities will have empowering ramifications beyond conferences and meetings. Youth who have positive mentoring relationships with a caring adult are more likely to be successful in school and beyond. Who knows how far they will go in their life once they start to believe in themselves and set high expectations? As Jonathan Mooney says, "It's not my fault that I have a disability, but it is my responsibility."

CHAPTER TEN

PROMOTING FAMILY PARTNERSHIPS

If we don't plant the right things, we will reap the wrong things. It goes without saying.

MAYA ANGELOU

For three decades, researchers have investigated the benefits of involving families in the education of their children. A substantial body of evidence confirms that when families and schools "partner in meaningful ways, children have more positive attitudes towards school, stay in school longer, have better attendance, and experience more school success" (U.S. Department of Education, 2015a). In addition, youths are more likely to graduate from high school and attain successful post-school outcomes if their families have been involved.

In 2004, the Appleseed Group was approached by the W.K. Kellogg Foundation to investigate how The No Child Left Behind Act could truly transform education for the students being left behind. After two years of research in 18 school districts in six states, they published It Takes A Parent: Transforming Education in the Wake of the No Child Left Behind Act. They summarize their conclusions as follows:

> It is clear that as a nation we have not emphasized or financially invested in parental involvement in ways that we should. The bold vision of NCLB (portraying parents as full participating partners) remains unfulfilled. A renewed focus on parental involvement is a powerful and exciting potential direction for education in the 21st Century. Indeed it could be a key to defeating persistent achievement gaps and engaging low-income and non-English speaking parents, too many of whom still stand outside the window looking in...Parental involvement is not a silver bullet, but is an important part of the solution. (Coleman et al., 2006)

The Appleseed report identified three overarching actions for parents in their partnerships with schools: a) become fully informed; b) support their youth to get the most out of his or her education; c) advocate for school improvement. Many of these recommendations have been incorporated into the reauthorized ESSA.

In December 2015, the U.S. Department of Education (2015) released a Draft Policy Statement on Family Engagement from the Early Years to the Early Grades. It defined family engagement as follows:

> We refer to "family engagement" as the systematic inclusion of families as partners in children's development, learning, and wellness. Engagement is enabled by positive relationships between families and staff in the institutions where children learn. The goal of family engagement is to support family wellness and children's learning and development.

Nobody disputes that schools and families should be partners in educating their children. It is generally known that we wouldn't have a special education law if families had not advocated in the 1970s. You would think that creating partnerships with families should be easily done. Not so. As I talk with school leaders during my initial consultation meeting, I typically ask what they want to accomplish through my work with them. They list improved professional collaboration, increased effectiveness of coteachers, and growth in measures of student progress. If I ask about their parent engagement, they say "Maybe in later years. Not now." I started wondering why.

I had noticed a similar phenomenon when I helped produce regional transition conferences as the state transition specialist. If I presented on the new transition components of the law, transition assessment, or ways to increase student engagement, the room was packed. If I presented on family engagement, there were only a handful in the audience. Why?

I think schools see family engagement as complex and overwhelming. In their groundbreaking book, *Beyond the Bake Sale*, Henderson and colleagues (2007) state, "The reality is that educators and parents have many beliefs, attitudes, and fears about each other that hinder their coming together to promote children's education." In my recent work, I have simplified family engagement for schools into three categories of action: (1) building a culture for family partnerships, (2) establishing effective outreach to families, and (3) empowering families to take action.

Building a Culture for Family Partnerships

As shown in Figure 10.1, the journey to building partnerships with families starts with a shift in educators' belief systems, their related behaviors, and the school power structure. Traditionally, schools take the lead with educational decisions, and they hold all the power. There is the unconscious assumption that teachers are the experts and the responsible party for the education of children. Administrators, teachers, and families think this way. We don't see it, but it influences how we interrelate. It also creates a barrier to powerful partnerships with families.

Figure 10.1

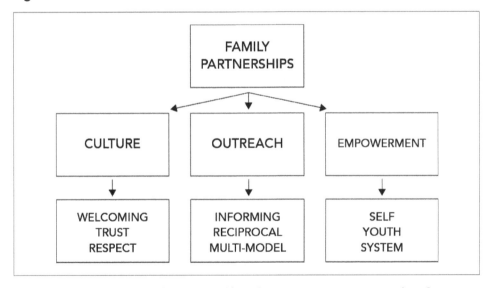

For example, I recently saw a self-evaluation questionnaire related to family engagement that a state technical assistance team had developed. One item on the list—We provide information to families about their role in the IEP process—made me pause. Do families only have the role that the school assigns to them? In your school who decides what roles a family can play?

I experienced that power hierarchy first hand when I attended my first IEP meeting as a parent. You would think that my background with special education would be an advantage, but at my son's first IEP meeting, I was dumbfounded about my role. I had participated in and even led hundreds of IEP meetings. I knew IEP meeting etiquette from enacting the script countless times. The parent should be officially welcomed. Then team members gave quick impersonal introductions as they shuffled folders.

Next came the required recitation of parent rights. Typically, a sideways glance at the parent would reveal their dread of this impersonal meeting where they were about to hear a list of their child's failings. Often, the team leader's words might convey reassurance, but after all, there was a job to do and a schedule to keep.

When I came to the table as a parent, I painfully experienced the inhumanity of that experience. Although I served that very team as the transition coordinator, Rick, the team leader, directed me to the parent seat and called me Mrs. Pleet. He explained that the psychologist and guidance counselor were still meeting with the previous parent and, in the interest of time, asked me if I would please share my concerns now so that we could get into the meat of the IEP when they joined us.

Without thinking, I said I would prefer to wait until they joined us since my concerns were about my son's social and emotional well-being. As I watched team members exchange glances, a prickly chill washed over me. Two minutes prior, these folks had been my colleagues and friends. Now I was on the other side of the "us" and "them" divide, and their faces became a blur of disapproval. I knew what they were thinking. I was going to be one of those problem parents. I was going to create a power struggle. I was going to get them behind on their schedule and create a class coverage nightmare.

At the time, I started feeling light headed. Compared to the stacks of stuffed folders in front of the professionals at the table, the slim manila folder at my place was pitifully inadequate. One corner of the tab had been bent at an awkward angle. My professional self felt the pressure to conform with established protocol and let them get on with the meeting.

But if I didn't stand up for my son at this meeting, who would? I gathered my courage during that meeting and later ones. I questioned proposed

IEP goals that I thought were unimportant and proposed alternative ones. However, I never got over that squeamish feeling at IEP meetings. Years later, I can now trace it to a power hierarchy. They were the authorities. They were in charge. I was supposed to comply. My speaking up felt like defiance. Their body language reinforced that they thought so, too.

Schools that commit to developing partnerships with families will confront this power hierarchy and consider how welcoming they are to families. Henderson and colleagues (2007) describe the following four types of schools in their stance to welcome families:

- **Fortress school:** Our school would be better if we had different students and different families.

- **Come if we call school:** Many of our families come if we invite them to perform specific tasks, like fundraisers, field trip chaperones, evening sports, and performances.

- **Open door school:** We have lots of family members here all the time for lots of activities that we have created for them. We keep them busy.

- **Partnership school:** We include families on our leadership team. Families partner with us in the education of their children.

School leaders and faculty will only make the journey to becoming a partnership school by reflecting on their attitudes and preconceived notions of what it means to foster family engagement. They examine how they build trusting, respectful relationships with families. They consider whether their practices imply that families are outsiders or whether they promote a sense of belonging.

Some schools now invite trained teams of parents and community members to conduct a structured school walkthrough. Parents don't visit their own child's school, but they have a chance to stop by the front office, stroll through the halls, and step into classrooms. Using outsider's eyes and a checklist, they evaluate the welcoming culture of the school. School leadership teams use the results to make improvements.

Using Covey's (2006) four cores of trust, every member of the staff from the front office secretary, cafeteria workers, bus drivers, custodial workers, teachers, guidance counselors, and administrators will look at the following characteristics:

- **Integrity:** Do we keep our word to families? Are our actions congruent with our professed values? If we promise to provide a safe and nurturing learning environment and stimulating, challenging instruction for all youth, can families trust us to do what it takes? If there are issues, do we honestly engage families in discussions about potential solutions?

- **Intent:** Have we clarified our values and intentions? Have we taken steps to publicize them to families and the community? I recently visited the Colonial School District in Delaware and was impressed with their new slogan, The Power of WE. On each stroke of WE, they have included key words that represent their values to make their intent crystal clear (see Figure 10.2).

- **Capabilities:** Have we taken steps to ensure that all faculty and staff have the knowledge, attitudes, and skills to interact positively with families? Many schools and districts provide professional development on topics such as multicultural competence and respectful dispute resolution. Teachers also need to know about the issues youth with disabilities and families will face as they transition into adult environments as well as options and services available during their transition years.

- **Results:** How well do we share news about our accomplishments? Families, as well as tax-paying community members who do not have children, are more likely to trust schools when they hear about youth who have succeeded and programs that are working. There is so much more to results than test scores.

Figure 10.2

Every state has at least one federal Parent Training and Information (PTI) center funded under the special education law. In addition, there are other centers and disability advocacy organizations established with a mission to inform families about their rights, responsibilities, and options within education. Increasingly, schools partner with such organizations to reach out to families.

Sometimes families become knowledgeable through association with these outside organizations, and they become empowered to advocate for their children. If they discover that schools are not especially welcoming or do not behave in ways that build trust, the result is friction between families and schools that can lead to official complaints, hearings, and expensive legal action.

Educators can avoid disgruntled parents if they reach out to them, truly listen to their stories with compassion, and include them as partners in decision making. As a parent, if I knew the team had my child's interests at heart, truly understood the issues my child faced at school and at home without judging me as a parent, and were authentically doing their best to address those issues, there was no way that I would consider filing an official complaint—even if it seemed that we weren't making progress. On the other hand, when I suspected the team was indifferent, impersonal, and simply following the letter of the law, I would not have hesitated to file a complaint the moment they were one day outside the legal timeline.

Most of my examples and discussion here has focused on families in the general population because that's where most of the research has been. Secondary schools and transition specialists who commit to building partnerships with families will start in the same place of intentionally creating a culture of shared ownership that is respectful of families' experiences, honors all perspectives, and builds trust.

Partnership during the transition years is even more critical because when students graduate high school, they also leave behind the professionals who have supported and managed their learning network of support. Families are often the ones who will help youths coordinate services and supports that they must advocate for.

Creating Effective Outreach to Families

Leaders and faculty in partnership schools approach family engagement systemically. They see families as insiders and valued allies who are part of the network of support contributing to the education of children. As they strategically design their outreach to families, they intentionally include activities that will provide multimodal information that families can use to participate as partners. Most of all, they establish reciprocal relationships, welcoming family contributions to their efforts.

We can learn a lot from investigating successful family engagement initiatives across the country. I was invited to represent parents of youth with disabilities in 2009 when the Institute for Education Leadership first assembled family engagement specialists from seven large urban school districts. Hearing the intentions and strategic actions of those committed individuals has impacted the trajectory of my career.

Michele Brooks, assistant superintendent of family and community engagement in Boston, was identified as a 2014 *Education Week* Leader to Learn From. I remember hearing her in the early years describe how she reached out to families living in poverty. Schools reported that the few families attending PTA meetings were not the ones who needed to be reached. She hitched a ride on neighborhood ice cream trucks, enthusiastically greeting families who gathered for evening treats. She asked where each of their children went to school and if they were satisfied with the quality of their education. Then she invited them to join her in a meeting the following week at the school to plan how families could improve their schools. Those parents showed up and were ready to help build stronger schools. As the project showed progress and worked with more schools, she repeated the process over several months all across the city.

Brooks' work in Boston has been replicated across the country as other educators planned creative ways to seek out families on their own turf. Some educators worked through leaders in faith-based institutions, and other educators worked with local community organizations. Their advice is to start with where your families are now. Which families are conspicuously absent when you hold events? Where can you find those families and how can you reach out to rebuild trust with them?

When I led a pre-conference workshop on family engagement at the National Division on Career Development and Transition Conference in Portland, Oregon in 2015, I wanted someone to serve on my panel who could represent multicultural families. I was referred to Ginger Kwan, Executive Director of Open Doors for Multicultural Families in Seattle. She described to our audience the one-on-one supports that her staff members, who are proficient in 22 languages, offer to diverse families of children with disabilities and the professionals that work with them. It was heartening to see faces light up as participants heard about her staff translating materials and attending IEP meetings with those families. What supports does your district offer for families and professionals seeking to bridge the divide created by language and cultural differences?

When planning outreach, some important questions to consider are "How can we reach families?," "What methods or multimodal approaches can we use?," and "Which ones would yield the best results?" Many schools ask the families to learn the answer to those questions. Typically, schools send print newsletters home and post news stories on their websites. Other options include the following:

- Email blasts sent to the family containing news bites about upcoming events and student accomplishments.

- Individual phone voicemail messages sent by a teacher or staff member with updates on their child's progress.

- Good news postcards sent home to announce a child's success.

- Voice messages recorded by individual teachers about school assignments or school events that families can retrieve at their convenience.

- Brief videos prepared by youth that inform families of school events or projects.

- Online or phone surveys to gather family perspectives on issues related to school programs and their children's education.

Whatever options your school selects, your school should consider potential access issues. Will any families need translations? If families do not have access to computers or the Internet, can your school make school computers available for them in the evening and on weekends? Since the growth of smartphones, more families now carry access to school information in their pockets. Schools just need to provide the right information at the right time.

Outreach begins with disseminating information, but if we are serious about engaging families as partners in efforts to improve the effectiveness of our educational system, it's not enough to simply reach out with information.

Empowering Families

Once families are invited and feel welcomed, what happens next will determine whether they return. Many of you have experienced the discomfort of back-to-school night, sitting in classrooms stuffed under too small children's desks while a teacher drones on about the expectations for the school year. Why do schools persist in this practice? In spite of my positive memories of years of success in school settings, I dread having to endure such torture. Think about those parents who experienced failure and dropped out of school. How can they tolerate being the passive target of a teacher in expert lecture mode? No wonder parents don't show up. I cringe when I remember how I subjected families to such an ordeal through most of my early years of teaching.

Many schools are now planning activities that engage families in sample learning activities where they and their children can participate together. Families who attend such workshops report that they use their new tools to support their own children's learning. But two other benefits have a more far-reaching impact. First, by their participation, families have communicated to their children that school work is important. When children hear that, it impacts their perspective of education. Second, families can spread the word to others at their workplaces and in the community about the fine work happening at their local schools. That positive publicity often ripples into other benefits for the school.

It's critical to remember that the purpose of engaging families is to support the development of children and their network of support. When schools and districts select activities for their family engagement plan, they should consider whether the options they consider will lead to opportunities for families to take meaningful action for increasing their own capacity, supporting their youth, and partnering with the school in improved educational outcomes.

First of all, schools that seek to build partnerships with families will consider how to expand the capacity of family members as valued members of the community. If adults seek ways to improve their own situations, it will improve the well-being of the community and impact the children. Some schools offer adult education classes on such topics as adult literacy, family budgeting, planning and cooking healthy meals, and English proficiency. These schools become a thriving community center.

A growing number of districts arrange to use college or community facilities during evenings or Saturday mornings to run Parent Academies or Parent Universities. A web search will reveal a variety of arrangements and offerings.

Patricia Spradley, the chief family and community engagement officer in Springfield, Massachusetts, runs a Parent Academy with classes on scrapbooking, yoga, English proficiency, literacy skills, computer literacy, budgeting, and real estate. These classes help families support their children's learning and build their own capacity. She asks families what they want, especially those silent families, and then finds a way to offer it with volunteer instructors from the community. In 2015, their Parent Academy offered over 400 classes with as many as 22 parents attending each one.

To build parents' capacity to support the learning of their children, some schools now establish teacher and parent teams to support academic learning. Teachers are prepared to lead a series of workshops that walk parents through typical academic learning activities. For example, parents are guided to read grade-level text, determine the author's position on an issue, and highlight key evidence used. Next, parents use a graphic organizer to plan an essay about that text and write their first draft. Finally, parents learn to use a rubric to evaluate the components of their composition. Through this process, they experience first hand the standards that their children are using in the classroom. Many parents report that after these workshops, they feel ready to support their children's learning at home.

Finally, schools that are truly committed to building partnerships with families will empower them to advocate for school improvement. Every state is required to have a special education advisory council with representation from families and adults with disabilities. Increasingly, schools welcome family representatives on school leadership teams and steering committees. Families who have been prepared with knowledge of key terms, the mission, and standard operating procedures of organizations can bring fresh perspectives to problem solving.

Secondary schools considering how to empower families of youth with disabilities can build on these ideas. These families can be empowered to support their young adults to develop executive skills and other routine behaviors that will be essential for adult life. Families can play critical roles in supporting the development of their teenagers' emerging independence and self-determination skills. In partnership with school and adult service providers, families can support youths to understand their disabilities, determine what accommodations and supports they need to be successful, and learn to advocate for themselves. How can your school create meaningful ways to empower families as partners?

Engaging families is becoming a national priority. At the same time, promising practices are emerging from the field and documented by research so schools don't have to re-invent the wheel. Schools that commit to building meaningful partnerships with families can organize their strategic plan into three action areas: (1) fostering a school culture of welcome, trust, and respect that makes families feel that they belong; (2) conducting outreach to inform families and build reciprocal, two-way relationships using multimodal and accessible approaches; and (3) planning engaging family activities that will empower them to build their own capacity, enable them to support their own youth's learning and development, and advocate for system improvement

CHAPTER ELEVEN

ENGAGING COMMUNITY PARTNERS

> We are like islands in the sea, separate on the surface but connected in the deep.
> **WILLIAM JAMES**

Inclusion of students with disabilities as I've described it in this book does not happen in a vacuum. Each year it seems that the expectations for public secondary education grows. Educators are now responsible for teaching rigorous curriculum, decreasing dropout rates, addressing multicultural issues, infusing technology, and being alert for homelessness, abuse, teen pregnancy, eating disorders, and substance abuse. The list grows each year, but none of the responsibilities are removed.

Community problems interfere and often prevent public schools from achieving their purpose of educating all students. As we focus on improvement that can be measured, such as test scores, attendance, and graduation rates, we sometimes overlook more important issues. We forget that we chose to work in education because we care about kids. We forget that what keeps us going is personal satisfaction from making a difference in someone else's life. Under political pressure to meet the needs of everyone, we lose the bonds of relationship. We become a dehumanized system with polarized "us versus them" thinking. This chapter is about integrating diverse stakeholders into a unified network of support that will strengthen everyone.

The Coalition for Community Schools, an alliance of more than 160 national, state, and local organizations, has united in efforts to broaden the base of responsibility for education across this country. In their report "Making the Difference: Research and Practice in Community Schools," Blank and colleagues (2003) describe the following seven community realities that challenge today's schools:

- **Cultural disconnects:** Nearly 20% of America's school age children speak a language other than English at home. While that number is expected to rise, 87% of America's teachers are white.

- **Too much unstructured time:** Several studies document that large numbers of children are unsupervised by adults. I was surprised to read the following—"Using data from the National Longitudinal Study of Adolescent Health, researchers concluded that time spent 'hanging out' with friends is a more accurate predictor of teenage risk behavior and school failure than income, race, or family structure."

- **Poverty:** The number of children living in poverty is increasing at an alarming rate. Children who are uncertain of basic needs like food and housing are less available for learning. The report states "National data shows a 30-point variance in test scores for every $10,000 change in household income."

- **Unaddressed health needs:** Even with new health insurance options, many families have no medical coverage, inadequate preventative care, and no dental care.

- **Transience:** High student mobility contributes to gaps in learning and social insecurity that lead to school failure and repeated grades. The disruption caused by new students interferes with the continuity of learning for the whole class.

- **Unsafe school environments:** One in four kids in the U.S. are bullied on a regular basis by physical bullying at school or cyberbullying online. More than half of bullying situations stop when a peer intervenes. Both students who experience bullying and those who are bullies are at increased risk for depression, anxiety, sleep difficulties, and school adjustment. Students receiving special education services are more likely to experience bullying and twice as likely to be told not to tattle if they report bullying (PACER, 2016).

- **Overburdened and under-resourced schools:** Schools in poverty areas with the most needs are more likely to have lower expectations for teacher competency and student mastery of rigorous curriculum.

Teachers are overwhelmed by these circumstances. Many teachers leave the profession, while others experience burnout. Maybe it's time to reach out to community partners for more than donations. Schools that engage partners can enhance their ability to produce graduates, including those students with disabilities who are ready to function in today's complex world. But it's not a one-way street. Schools can contribute to neighborhoods and help them become nurturing places for children, families, and communities to flourish. Everybody wins.

Figure 11.1

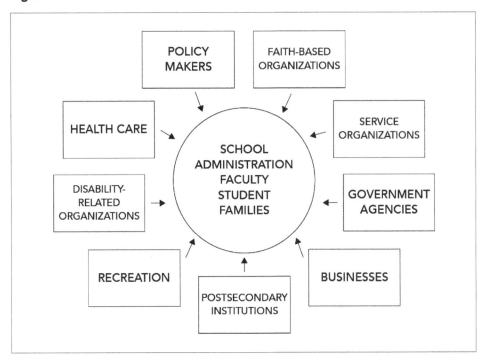

Figure 11.1 displays the range of community resources that are potential partners with schools. I urge you to use this partial list as a conversation starter. What organizations could be on the list in your local area? What companies and organizations employ the parents in your school? For example, consider the following community partners:

- **Policymakers:** Legislators, governors, mayors, school boards, and advisory boards

- **Faith-based organizations:** Churches, synagogues, mosques, faith-based alliances, and charities

- **Service organizations:** Lions' Club, Jaycees, Habitat for Humanity, Toys for Tots, Meals on Wheels, senior citizens organizations, fraternities, sororities, and foundations

- **Government agencies:** Education, housing, transportation, fire, police, and waste management

- **Businesses:** Local employers, business roundtables, chambers of commerce, and licensing boards

- **Postsecondary institutions:** Universities, colleges, career and literacy centers, adult education, apprenticeships, and researchers

- **Recreation groups:** Professional sports, YMCA, Boys & Girls Clubs, martial arts, theaters, arts, sports, yoga, zoo, libraries, museums, and online meetups

- **Disability-related organizations:** Advocacy groups (e.g. Arc, CHADD, and Autism Speaks), state agencies (vocational rehabilitation, developmental disabilities, mental and health), and adult service providers

- **Health care organizations:** Hospitals, doctors, therapists, dentists, substance abuse centers, and public health centers

While each of the organizations on your list has its own vision, mission statement, and standard operating procedures, many of them would benefit from contributing to improved educational outcomes. Most schools have a few community partners that have donated to school projects or sponsored events. I remember when my children were in school, they could earn coupons at the local pizza establishment by reading books at home. It worked! They were motivated to read, and I was glad to use their coupons for a pizza night out.

Those business sponsor arrangements have their place, but across the country schools are collaborating with organizations to take it to the next level. It's not easy. It takes work and commitment, but schools that engage in strategic community partnerships report worthwhile benefits. The Coalition for Community Schools report begins with the following quotation:

A community school is not just another program being imposed on a school. It embodies a way of thinking and acting that recognizes the historic central role of schools in our communities—and the power of working together for a common good. Educating our children, yes, but also strengthening our families and communities so that, in turn, they can help make our schools even stronger and our children even more successful (Blank, Melaville, & Shah, 2003).

Their publication summarizes the following four advantages of forging community partnerships:

- Student learning in academic and nonacademic development
- Family engagement in support of their children's learning success
- School effectiveness measured by increased teacher satisfaction, more positive school environment, and greater community support
- Community vitality through better use of school buildings, heightened community pride, increased security, and better rapport among students and residents

Community schools are described as hubs of the community, "open to everyone—all day, every day, evenings, and weekends...community schools knit together inventive, enduring relationships among educators, families, volunteers and community partners." This report emphasizes that the establishment of community schools allows teachers to teach and principals to be instructional leaders. Community schools draw on the expertise and resources of community partners to serve as social workers, health and wellness specialists, and police officers.

I recently visited an urban middle school that had been identified as persistently dangerous. They reached out to families, recreational facilities, and businesses to build partnerships. Now, the local YMCA provides tutoring and sports activities for students after school for free or at a reduced cost. Volunteers from local businesses are now trained reading partners. These volunteers come from local businesses during their lunch break to provide one-on-one reading interventions to students. Parents I spoke with shared that becoming a reading partner helped them support their younger children at home learn to read. This community partnership addresses more than one purpose within a few activities. More importantly, it contributed to the school's and the community's pride and belonging.

Focus Areas for Community Partnerships

School and community partnerships should be customized to meet the unique needs of each school and community. Stakeholders engaged in strategic planning will want to consider first what they want to accomplish with their partnerships. Epstein and colleagues (2009) categorized community partnerships into four focus areas: (1) student centered, (2) family centered, (3) school centered, and (4) community centered.

Creating Student-Centered Practices

Student-centered practices are focused on student gains in learning, personal development, enrichment, and motivation. These partnerships expand the school's capacity to provide tutoring, mentoring, job shadowing and awareness, student incentives, enrichment activities, field trips, and scholarships. Activities are grounded in the belief that students are more likely to succeed in school and life if they are physically, socially, and emotionally competent. Teachers who are focused on common core standards will find it challenging to address these bigger issues with each child in the course of daily instruction. This is where community partnerships can come in.

For example, in the federally funded 21st Century Community Learning Centers initiative, community and faith-based organizations work in partnership with schools to provide after-school and summer learning opportunities for children. These centers, established over the last decade in all 50 states, have led to improved student behavior and achievement through creative ways to support individual learning, as well as alternative entry points for family members to support their student's learning (Little, 2013).

Some schools use business partners as mentors for at-risk youth. These initiatives increase attendance and graduation rates and decrease discipline referrals. Many schools are using faith-based or neighborhood ethnic organizations to help them address cultural differences in their student body. Christopher Chatmon, a 2015 Education Week Leader to Learn From, was recognized for the Manhood Development Program he established in the Oakland, California Unified School District for African American male students. The program matched students with Black mentors from the community for activities supporting their future potential.

Part of my job description as a transition coordinator was to supervise students with disabilities in work-based learning experiences. I remember working with Sam, a 17-year-old senior with very active ADHD. After being fired from several jobs, he was excited to land a job as a busboy and dishwasher in a burger and ice cream shop in the local mall. I had worked with his manager, Sharie, before with previous students and knew her to be someone who would give second chances.

On Sam's second day on the job, I perched on a bench in the mall where I could watch him work. I saw Sam pick up a glass, bend over the dishwashing station behind the counter, and bob his head to his headphones. With his ever-present grin, he dried his hands on his apron and dashed the long loop around the counter, weaving in front of waitresses balancing plates of food to put that one glass in its place on the rack. I sat still long enough to see him repeat himself with three dishes, oblivious of his dangling shirt tail or the tables he passed that needed clearing.

I stood up, planning how I would help him to learn some critical life lessons about responsibility and earning trust. Sharie saw me and came out of the shop towards me. After friendly greetings, I asked her how I could help with Sam. When she hesitated, I reassured her with my observations. "Well, I can see that he needs to tuck in his shirt, wash more than one dish at a time, be aware that waitresses get right of way, and look out for tables that need clearing." She smiled, exhaled, and nodded. "What I want to know," I added, "is what you want to handle and where you want me to step in."

We worked it out. I would give Sam an overview of why I would fire him based on what I saw. Then she would work with him on how to improve. The opportunity for Sam to grow and learn as an employee and an adult was a valuable contribution from this business partner. What he learned on the job spilled over to other areas of his life. Soon teachers started noticing that he became more conscientious in his appearance and his class assignments.

Developing Family-Centered Strategies

With family-centered strategies, community organizations provide resources and expertise within the school to support parents and the whole family's capacity. These can include parenting workshops, family fun and learning nights, child care, GED preparation, adult education, nutrition, and crisis counseling. For families of youth with disabilities, they would also offer disability related information and referrals to advocacy organizations and adult service providers. When staffed by community organizations and volunteers, they provide supports to families beyond what typical school staff have the time and capabilities to offer.

These programs and activities focus on expanding the knowledge and skills of families so that they can be more effective in their functions of providing for and nurturing the development of their children. Even more, these approaches build families' social capital. As they come into contact with educators, businesses, organizations, and their neighbors, they build relationships with individuals who they can turn to when needed. They weave a network of neighborhood supports where families become available to each other for present and future problem solving related to employment, health, transportation, parenting, and well-being. These practices go far beyond providing a Family Center where families and volunteers can grab a cup of coffee, browse reference materials, and hang their coats. Frequently those family centers are a vacant gesture without the commitment to partnership.

At the national Family and Community Engagement Conference in 2014, I overheard three district leaders share that they had closed their school-based family centers and reassigned their family and community ombudsmen positions. They said that administrators and teachers used that position to save themselves from dealing with problem families and redirected any family or community concerns to the ombudsmen. By eliminating those positions in schools, the district leaders clarified that partnerships were instead the responsibility of all faculty, staff, and administrators. Family-centered supports set the groundwork for families to resolve their issues with teachers and administrators directly. The offerings at Parent Universities and Parent Academies I described in Chapter 10 could be expanded with community partners.

Developing School-Centered Approaches

It is in a community's economic interest to have strong, safe schools. When businesses investigate regions to expand or relocate their operations and bring more jobs, they frequently research the quality of the local schools.

Entrepreneur Media (2015) notes that of the 10 things to consider when choosing a location for a business, the second item is location demographics. This includes determining whether the community has a stable economic base and whether the community supports the needs of their workforce. For this last aspect, they ask, "What skills do you need, and are people with those talents available? Does the community have the resources to serve their needs? Will your employees find the schools, recreational opportunities, culture, and other aspects of the community satisfactory?"

To support the problem of truancy, local businesses can post signs that students are only welcome during nonschool hours. Partnerships might make contributions to a natural habitat or community garden that could benefit student learning opportunities as well as beautify the school. I visited a middle school with powerful business partners that paid for a renovated media center and a high tech science lab that was used for adult evening education. Everyone using the building benefitted from those improvements.

Inviting Community-Centered Programs and Outreach

Community partnerships often repurpose school buildings, long vacant in the evenings, weekends, and summer, into vibrant community centers. They create places where community members can engage in lifelong learning with offerings in adult literacy, English proficiency, financial management, computer skills, nutrition, and wellness. Some neighborhoods establish community wellness centers in their schools to provide medical, dental, mental health counseling, crisis intervention, and health care referrals for the community.

Community partnerships can support all families, not just those with children in the school, to build social capital as they meet with their neighbors and community leaders for recreational activities and to address pressing issues like crime prevention, teenage pregnancy, substance abuse, and community beautification. As individuals in the community become less isolated and establish a network of support, they are more likely to draw upon those relationships to solve family and community problems that benefit all stakeholders.

Students who participate in community service learning opportunities give back to their schools and communities while increasing their network of positive adult role models. Youth with disabilities who are included in these schoolwide efforts benefit from normalized associations focused on their abilities and contributions to common goals. In addition, teenagers with adult mentors in the community increase their awareness of possible careers and pathways to achieve them.

Superintendent Tiffany Anderson, another 2015 Education Week Leaders to Learn From, was concerned that over 90% of students in her St. Louis high school qualified for free and reduce-priced lunch. She pulled together business and community leaders. Their partnership created a food pantry that serves over 200 people every two weeks. The high school students stock the shelves and distribute it directly to community members who line up. Think of the life lessons and leadership opportunities for youth participating in projects like this.

Forging Partnerships

Strong, effective, community partnerships don't just happen. Schools and communities must come together strategically to target mutual needs, identify available human, material, and financial resources, and establish trusting arrangements to make it all work. Suppose we start with the assumption that every family and every community organization has assets to contribute to strong neighborhood schools. Our question is how do we leverage those assets? How do we empower local businesses and community agencies to contribute their resources to expand our capacity to provide a rich educational experience for our youth? Several prominent organizations provide guidance on the process of establishing effective partnerships. I have combined several frameworks into the following steps:

Step 1: Create a Shared Vision

The school principal's support for these efforts is crucial to establishing the intent of the group as well as sustaining activities in the long term. The principal doesn't have to maintain the lead. A school and family advisory committee will want to invite potential partners with common goals and a commitment to strengthening the school and community. What business or organizational leaders in your community could contribute to your solutions?

Partnerships are grounded in the assumption that all contributing members have value. Right from the start, partners establish a climate for two-way communication where all parties' perspectives are welcomed, respected, and considered. When families, community representatives, and school leaders all collaborate to create a shared vision, the result is a "clearly articulated purpose and statement of desired results" (Blank, Melaville, & Shah, 2003). Bear in mind that simplicity is better for first efforts. Remember that community partnerships should decrease, not increase, the burden on school personnel.

Step 2: Grow Partnership Spirit

Each of the partners, whether they represent families, the school, or the range of community organizations, is valuable to the partnership because of differences. They contribute their knowledge about children, their awareness of neighborhood circumstances, their professional and business expertise, and their experience with how their own system operates. In order for them to work together, however, they may need background knowledge of each other. Simple vocabulary may have alternate meanings for those coming from different orientations.

Most people think they know a teacher's responsibilities from their memories as a student. They get a surprise from shadowing a teacher for a day. Conversely, teachers frequently have little knowledge of employers' expectations. Years ago, I participated in a business enterprise course sponsored by my school district and the local chamber of commerce. Every Wednesday after school for 10 weeks, we toured a different community business. We listened to human resources directors explain entry-level skills and reasons why their young employees were fired. I realized the damage we do when we say, "You earned a C. Not so bad. You can do better next time." A boss would have fired them for C-level work. Understanding their world made it easier for me to partner with business leaders. How well do your partners understand each other's perspectives?

These walk-in-your-shoes activities can establish communication and trusting relationships. Community partnerships also agree on ground rules for communication, record keeping, decision making, and procedures for working through differences. Some invite neutral partners to act as facilitators.

Step 3: Plan Strategically

Once the partnership advisory group has created the shared vision and identified the targeted outcomes, the next step is to develop a specific plan. If the group has taken time with Step 2, the partners will have increased awareness of each other, making it easier to negotiate offers or requests. Some groups begin with an open brainstorming session where any ideas can be shared freely without judgment or criticism that often lead to creative solutions.

Like all strategic plans, the group should clarify partners' roles, provision of needed resources and who will pay, an implementation timeline with benchmarks, including training and evaluative measures. Often partners recognize the need to invite others to the table to expand their expertise and resources.

Step 4: Implement, Evaluate, Reflect, and Celebrate

Once the new or expanded activities are launched, the advisory group meets periodically to problem solve unforeseen circumstances and evaluate the effectiveness of the activity or program to meet the identified need. Often it is helpful to hear first-hand testimony of a student, family, or community partner about their experience of advantages, challenges, and perspectives on possible improvement.

Finally, these groups should plan celebrations. It is no small feat when partners come together and share their resources, experience, and expertise for a common purpose, especially if the targeted gains are achieved. The celebration can be as simple as a ceremony awarding certificates or as big as a banquet. The most important element is acknowledging those who contributed to the new practice and achieved remarkable results. As Blank and colleagues (2003) said, "Community schools illustrate what can happen when the forces of community triumph over indifference."

※❀❀※

Regardless of where your school is now or where you hope to be, every time you engage a new partner, you strengthen your school network. Think of each partnership as a thread in the web of support for your youth, teachers, administrators, families, and the broader community.

Families, schools, and community organizations all win when they join together in a commitment to building stronger schools. Students benefit by additional human and material resources to enrich their learning opportunities. Families benefit from investments in their own capacities and from joining with others to support their children. Schools benefit from supplemental investments in their efforts to educate children. Businesses benefit from a better prepared workforce. Everyone gains when systems become humanized and relationships are forged that reverse the effects of isolation.

As the initial quote from William James states, "...we are connected in the deep." We just have to make those connections visible and intentional. By including youth with disabilities and their families in these connections, we have created a network to increase their chances of post-school success.

CHAPTER TWELVE

STRATEGIC SCHOOL CHANGE

> The future is not some place we are going but one we are creating.
> The paths are not to be found, but made, and the activity of making
> them changes both the maker and the destination.
>
> **JOHN SHEAR**

My heart aches for school leaders and teachers who are incessantly bombarded by school improvement initiatives. When I ask how things are going, their answers reveal how overwhelmed and drained they are by the immensity of the tasks ahead of them. They list all the initiatives as separate projects—integrating technology, striving for rigorous standards, individualizing instruction, not to mention addressing student needs related to disability, poverty, homelessness, teenage pregnancy, substance abuse, and English acquisition. When school change is seen as separate, fragmented initiatives, teachers feel the need to prioritize their efforts towards implementing the one or two that appear easiest to incorporate into their current practices. That does not produce sustainable school transformation.

Three years ago, I had a wake-up call about our dysfunctional approach to school change. Knowing that fly-by professional development would not change teachers' practices, I had made prior arrangements with the principal when he invited me to conduct a workshop. He had planned to introduce me with his endorsement of the initiative and his expectations for teachers. At the last minute, the principal was called to district offices and the assistant principal was dealing with an upset parent. That left me to introduce myself and to look into the faces of overwhelmed teachers and ask them to try one more thing. It was a thankless job for all of us.

That day was a turning point for me. I immersed myself in research about school change that confirmed what I already suspected. Change cannot happen with one standalone workshop. Since then, I have resolved to only provide professional development that is integrated in a long-range plan for systemic improvement, including support for teachers as they develop new competencies and make personal adjustments to the change.

How Do We Approach Change?

All of us live with change on a daily basis. Although we are most comfortable when we can keep things as they are, we also embrace change. Who would prefer to return to the days without the convenience of computers, smartphones, internet, and efficient modes of travel?

The National Academy for Academic Leadership (2016) notes that change falls into two categories. First order change requires a new way of operating that adds a few skills to our present competencies. It means trying to do current practices in a better way. That change is reversible if we find it doesn't produce the results we wanted. Reflective teachers initiate first order change all the time.

Second order change (also called paradigm shift) requires that we learn an entirely new set of competencies. In a paradigm shift many of our previous ways of operating are irrelevant and useless. We use a new way of thinking to operate in the new situation, and once launched, we cannot return to the prior situation. In short, "change redefines proficiency" (Evans, 2015).

Spiro (2009) reminds us that this second type of change "...is about a deliberate disruption of the status quo. While the need for change will often be apparent to many or most of those affected, opposition, resistance and unanticipated consequences are all likely to emerge....Even positive change can be stressful. An effective change leader can maximize the opportunities of change while minimizing the risks."

Today with looming pressures of legislated requirements for accountability casting huge shadows, school leaders and faculty are bombarded from all sides with experts eager to share their latest evidence-based approaches to cure their problems. When asked, teachers confess they're overwhelmed with too many ideas. The intent of this book is to integrate multiple proven approaches into a unified system for different responsibility domains. Schools that use a common sense, simplified and, strategic approach to school reform with a sensitivity to participants' stressful reactions to change will have a better chance of engaging stakeholders and achieving lasting success.

Setting the Stage

In my nearly five decades of experience, I have been involved in countless school reform initiatives. I experienced first hand the changes brought about by the first special education law, open space middle schools, advocacy efforts for inclusion, and new transition requirements. I've partnered with schools, districts, and states in their initiatives to expand family engagement practices and increase efficacy of special educators. I will focus on whole-school change here, but these principles can be easily translated to the work of teams, departments, districts, or states.

The impetus for change could come from new federal or state legislation or new district policies, shifting student demographics, or the gap between targeted educational outcomes and current results. Whether or not schools have a choice about participation in the change, stakeholders always have a choice about their degree of commitment. Change agents understand the importance of ground work to set the stage for transformation by engaging stakeholders and building a learning community.

Engaging Stakeholders

Ultimately, most school change will be implemented by teachers with the support of administrators and endorsement of families and community members. One of the biggest mistakes that schools and districts make is to delay engaging these stakeholders. When I hear principals or district leaders say that they want to work out all the kinks in their plan before presenting it to the school board or faculties or families, I know they have lost an important part of their leverage, not to mention losing out on the possibility of more good ideas.

Stakeholders need and want to be included in initial conversations to contribute to decisions about desired outcomes, emerging problem patterns from their perspectives, solution options, action plans, and progress evaluations. Their involvement is central to the success of any plans for change, but when they are excluded from the planning, it is difficult to secure their buy-in later. Of course, it would be unmanageable to have all stakeholders at the drawing board. But a leader who makes a concerted effort to include representatives of all stakeholder groups and uses transparent methods of management increases general trust in the process (Covey, 2006).

Evans (2015) states that practitioners will fall into three levels of commitment to change—educators who make it happen, help it happen, and let it happen. In the course of implementing the plan, the change leaders will first engage key stakeholders whose endorsement will influence others' buy-in. Sometimes they begin with a pilot project by encouraging early adopters who thrive on innovative opportunities to experiment with the new approach. If the plan is structured so that they can have an early win, they can sharetheir results with the rest of the faculty. They can also be used as peer mentors as others come on board.

The Innovative Schools Network uses this approach, encouraging schools to invite teachers, families, and students to apply for participation in a proposed innovative zone in their school. This zone, led by teacher leaders, will create an experiment in personalized learning outside the typical constraints of bell schedules, isolated subjects, and teacher-made assessments. Instead, students and teacher advisors will work together to design learning experiences that are truly student centered and guided by student self-assessment and peer collaborative learning.

There is no one approach that works in all schools. Leaders will have to facilitate the plan's development to fit the individual characteristics of their staff and the demands of the proposed change. All the experts agree, however, that sustainable change won't happen without engaging the hearts of those involved. Evans (2015) stated it this way, "One of the central lessons we think we have learned about previous rounds of innovationis that they failed because they didn't get at fundamental, underlying, systemic features of school life: they didn't change the behaviors, norms, and beliefs of practitioners."

Establishing a Learning Community

Hutchens (2011) describes learning as a journey. He says it is "a discipline. It's a way of looking at the world. It's about growth and discovery." Further, he says, "learning is continually enhancing one's capability to create, think, relate, and act in productive ways. Learning is innate. You—and your organization—are learning all the time, whether you intend to or not. The big question is, "What can we do to trigger this innate learning ability in ways that help us achieve the things that matter to us the most?"

Hutchens (2011) notes that learning communities foster the following markers in their members:

- **New skills and capabilities:** Members are able to do things they couldn't do before.

- **New awareness and sensibilities:** Members use a systems approach and question basic underlying assumptions that were obvious to everyone to create a new mental model of how the world works.

- **New attitudes and beliefs:** As a result of learning, members change their beliefs about what is possible and those beliefs fundamentally alter future behavior.

I have especially enjoyed my consultation over the last few years in one charter middle school that embodies the principles of a learning community. Every time I return, I am greeted by teachers who can't wait to tell me new ways they implemented the strategies from my last visit. When I shared a method for differentiating instruction, they invented a way to incorporate technology. When I gave them guidelines for collaborative learning, they reorganized their stations activities. Their creativity and enthusiasm for new learning is contagious. It's not surprising that their students, who are all inner-city scholars, display that same eagerness for learning.

Anticipate Resistance

We all know that there will always be some who resist change. Resistance is a normal reaction to change. As schools contemplate change initiatives, they should consider who will push back and why. By anticipating resistance and the underlying reasons for it, leaders can create ways to address those issues. For example, Mr. Lyman, who earned a master's degree in special education, may not want a coteaching assignment because he has heard horror stories about special educators being treated like assistant teachers. Mrs. Yin may be worried about the proposed inclusive middle school program because her son has been bullied in unsupervised settings. Both of these stakeholders have valid concerns that must be addressed before new initiatives will have their support.

Evans (2015) describes a duality of change that brings humor to the situation. We all see benefits for other people changing, especially those who are leading the change. But we resist "the humiliation of becoming a raw novice at a new trade after having been a master craftsman at an old..." (Kaufman, 1971 as cited in Evans, 2015). He encourages us to view resistance "as part of the solution, not just part of the problem; it demands the attention and respect of all who seek innovation."

The Satisfaction Cycle

I use a responsive model to guide common sense school transformation that I call the satisfaction cycle (see Figure 12.1). These seven steps blur together throughout the process, rather than serving as clear demarcations in time. For example, while exploring options, stakeholders may want to revisit values. School strategic planning teams find this model a useful way to progress in school transformation.

Figure 12.1

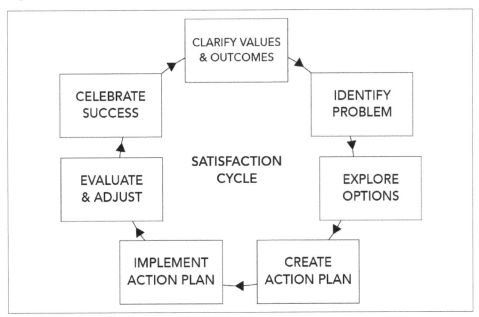

Clarify Values and Outcomes

Engaging stakeholders and establishing a learning community provide a background context to enable school change. They create a learning culture that can be cultivated as a fertile ground for school transformation. The first step in the change process is to clarify and explicitly state the school's values. Perhaps the team will need to dust off the school vision statement and invite stakeholder perspectives about whether their vision is inspirational for current times.

Next the strategic planning team will identify the desired outcomes that would indicate that the school values are being realized. "Without compelling, clearly defined results, organizational learning does not take place. (It also won't happen if the intended results fail to tap into people's deepest aspirations)" (Hutchens, 2011).

Identify Problems

Whether the new initiative is internally or externally motivated, the strategic planning team will articulate the specific problems to be addressed. After examining gaps between desired outcomes and current performance, they will look for patterns to identify what is missing in their current practice. They will prepare a summary of the specific data that will be used to gauge the effectiveness of the initiative. Some will want to target graduation and dropout statistics or increase the percentage of graduates who succeed in higher education. Others may want to improve the percentage of students with disabilities who are successfully included in general education classrooms, growth in student social-emotional behavior, or the effectiveness of special educators in new inclusive roles. Perhaps the team decides to tackle the number of families currently participating in engagement efforts or their capacity to support their youth during the transition years.

The focus of the stated problems will be a collective sense of purpose rather than a prescribed set of actions to be taken. For example, a school can declare, "We will reduce the dropout rate for students with disabilities" rather than "We will create a mentoring program." Evans (2015) states "It is now widely accepted that a clear sense of purpose is vital to productivity and especially to innovation, that leaders invigorate performance and inspire commitment to change by engaging their people in the pursuit of shared goals."

Explore Options

There are choices to be made in implementing any change. Who will be involved? What materials, strategies, or approaches will be used? When stakeholders' input is incorporated into the plan, they are more likely to be committed to its success.

Dean Ray Lorion of Towson University once told me that an effective leader tells people up front how their input will be used. There is nothing more frustrating for stakeholders than to generate lots of ideas for change that are not welcome or considered. Lorion gave the following three possibilities:

1. We need to make a change, and I need your help researching all our options.

2. We need to make a change, and I need your thoughts on whether we should go with these options A, B, or C.

3. We need to make THIS change, and I need your help deciding exactly how to make it work.

School leaders and teams have some critical considerations as they select effective practices to address their issues related to special education. The Council for Exceptional Children's Division for Research published recommendations for the special education practices (Odom et al., 2005). To begin, strategies must be based on scientific research using one of the four following types of acceptable design methodologies or mixed methods:

1. **Experimental group design:** A study that involved implementing an intervention with an experimental group and not with a control group, with subjects randomly assigned to control variables. Gersten and colleagues (2005) describe rigorous standards for establishing the context of the study, describing the subject groups, the intervention, as well as collecting, analyzing, and evaluating data with validity and reliability.

2. **Correlational design:** "Quantitative, multi-subject designs in which participants have not been randomly assigned to treatment conditions" (Thompson et al., 2005) where researchers use statistics and logic to identify relational (i.e., causative) patterns between a treatment and a result.

3. **Single-subject design:** A study of one or more participants, focusing on each subject individually, in which the performance of the subject(s) is described before and after an intervention using variables that are specific, measurable, and replicable by others (Horner et al., 2005).

4. **Qualitative design:** "A systematic approach to understanding qualities or the essential nature, of a phenomenon within a particular context" (Brantlinger et al., 2005) through interviews or intensive observation.

Odom and colleagues (2005) describe how the complexities of special education make it the "hardest-to-do science." In most scientific research, scientists control all the variables except the one(s) they want to test. In education, it is impossible to control most variables because of differences between students, even with the same diagnosis, not to mention the variability of teachers, diverse classrooms, school environments, family conditions, and leadership. The list goes on. As a result, researchers must ask specific research questions. Will this practice work with this population in this situation if conducted in this exact manner? The heterogeneous nature of a classroom will make it challenging to establish equivalent groups. Ethical concerns arise when researchers decide which students will be included in an experimental group and which ones will not receive the intervention in a control group. Just because a research study concluded that a practice worked, the question remains—Will it work with our kids with these teachers in our school?

Evidence-based practices meet rigorous criteria established by professional organizations such as the What Works Clearinghouse. Teams of experts review research studies to determine whether the practice is "supported by multiple, high-quality, experimental, or quasi-experimental (often including single-case research) studies demonstrating that the practice has a meaningful impact on consumer (e.g., student) outcomes" (Cook & Odom, 2013).

Selecting the appropriate practice to fit a school's needs is no easy matter. As Cook and Odom (2013) say, "EBP [evidence-based practices] are not guaranteed to work for everyone. No practice will work for every single student; this is a reality of education … of which special educators are keenly aware." An evidence-based practice often has some percentage of students who are nonresponders to the intervention. Some practices are not labeled evidence-based practices because research has shown that they are ineffective, while others simply do not have sufficient research yet.

Once the practice has been selected, the challenges continue. School personnel will encounter additional issues during implementation, such as the following scenarios described by Cook and Odom (2013):

> Implementing and sustaining new practices involves a host of complex and interrelated problems, including issues related to the practice being promoted (e.g., relevance and fit to target environment, efficiency, and practicality), users (e.g., available time, mistrust of research, knowledge of EBPs, and skills), and the institutional context (e.g., available resources, organizational structures and culture, staffing, coaching, training, and administrative support).

In many fields of practice, there has been growing interest in implementation science, "The scientific study of methods to promote the systematic uptake of research findings and other evidence-based practices into routine practice" (Eccles & Mittman, 2006). As this field grows, it will provide guidance to educational practitioners as they bridge the gap between identifying evidence-based practices and implementing them within school environments. Simply replicating a practice found somewhere else without considering how to adapt it for the students, professionals, and learning environment in a school is unlikely to be successful. Through investigating implementation science publications, school leaders can gain valuable perspectives into issues such as balancing fidelity of implementation with flexibility and scaling-up implementation efforts.

Create an Action Plan

Once the options have been evaluated, the strategic planning team will create an action plan. In essence, the plan answers the question "What will we do or put in place to achieve the results we desire?" This is the part of school change that leaders find most comfortable. We are all accomplished at writing detailed plans. In addition to the activities, timeline, responsibilities, and benchmark evaluation components, schools committed to lasting change will include guiding ideas and structures for professional learning.

Build Guiding Ideas. Hutchins (2011) explains, "Guiding ideas include the beliefs, assumptions, and values that we hold about what it will take to create a particular desired result." An action plan should explicitly state the new guiding ideas that may challenge our long held beliefs, such as "All students can learn," "Students with disabilities can learn in a general education classroom," "Bullying behavior can be prevented," or "Special educators' main responsibility is to foster students' self-efficacy." What are the big ideas guiding your proposed changes?

Develop Structures for Learning. The plan will also include the structures that will be in place to support professional learning throughout the action plan. Some examples of structures from Hutchens (2011) include the following:

- **Meetings:** This structure specifies who will attend, how often, what will be discussed, and how they will foster team learning.

- **New materials, technology, or software:** This structure describes new materials to be used and how practitioners will be oriented to their use.

- **Professional development:** This structure outlines new knowledge and skills that will be needed, who will provide it, and how it will be personalized.

- **Ongoing support for practice and reflection:** This structure describes what opportunities are available for experimentation, reflection, sharing, and coaching.

Hutchins (2011) warns us, however, that an action plan without a learning culture is not enough. He said, "People and groups who focus most of their energies here may find that they can indeed produce their desired results, but not for long. Over time, motivation and ability to sustain the changes will lag."

Implement an Action Plan

Leaders who want to foster long-lasting change need to be aware of the natural human progression through the change process, keeping in mind that each person will be on his own journey at his own pace. Hutchens (2011) summarizes the issue as follows:

How will we pursue our goals in a way that engages people's hearts and spirits? This is the mysterious and oft-ignored 'people piece' of the framework. When we create environments where people choose to enroll themselves in the doing, we create the possibility for sustainable, transformational change. Note that you can't make someone engage in the deep learning cycle; people can only choose to enter into it themselves.

Evans (2015) informs us that during paradigm change skilled leaders guide teachers through the following sequence of tasks:

- **Unfreezing:** Increase the fear of not trying, reduce the fear of trying, and make it safe to experiment and express authentic feelings and experiences. Leaders will use a combination of persuasive information that creates dissatisfaction with current results. They will also encourage teachers to alter their behavior to align with shared ideals and a reinforced belief that we can do this together.

- **Moving from loss to commitment:** Make the change meaningful by emphasizing the core values of teachers' mission that initially prompted them to become educators. During this stage, teachers will experience deeply personal reactions to giving up old, familiar ways of operating. They must each work through their resistance to change and make their own meaning of the new initiative at their own rate. Personal contact with change leaders is needed to assuage their loss of prior status and to assimilate new thinking.

- **Moving from old competence to new competence:** Develop new behaviors, skills, beliefs, and ways of thinking. Teachers willingly engage in training that is coherent (i.e., organized in a logically, sequential way), continuous (i.e., with opportunities for safe practice and feedback), and personal (i.e., tailored to each teacher's prior background and comfort level). Trainers and coaches play an ongoing role with teachers' evolution of new practices and "...training must include continuing opportunities for teachers to consider, discuss, argue about, and work through changes in their assumptions" (Evans, 2015).

- **Moving from confusion to coherence:** Realign structures, functions, and roles. As teachers begin to implement new practices, leaders support them to resolve uncertainty about responsibilities, relationships, and standard procedures. They provide clear guidelines for decision making by determining which decisions are already made by leaders and which ones are open for teams or individuals.

- **Moving from conflict to consensus:** Generate broad support for change. While realistically, some faculty may still resist implementation of the change, "...the building of commitment among a critical mass of staff ranks among the most important goals change agents can set for themselves" (Evans, 2015). Leaders will target the staff members who are critical to the initial success of the change. Evans (2015) further states "... when innovation reaches this critical mass and has recruited a range of advocates, change acquires a momentum of its own and moves into the mainstream of discussion, perception, and practice."

School leaders who are aware of these tasks and provide personalized support to each teacher are more likely to achieve sustainable change. I have lived through strategic change initiatives that followed this sequence of tasks and have fond memories of the bonds that formed within our ranks. Unfortunately, we all have plenty of experiences where we rushed through or skipped steps. Those initiatives produced firmly entrenched resistance and little change.

Provide Professional Development. Frequently, school change involves professional development as teachers move from old to new competence. It can be provided by respected, in-house faculty members, district personnel, or outside experts. As I mentioned in the opening of this chapter, professional development will only be effective when it is provided as part of a systemic approach. Ahead of time, the principal must prepare the faculty to understand the purpose of the workshop and have clear expectations for how they will apply what they learn.

Before I provide professional development to a school, I've learned to gather background about the participants. The more I know about current practices and where my workshop fits within the school improvement plan, the more I can tailor it to the specific needs of the faculty. Lately, I've been experimenting with online modules and webinars to personalize supports. As new technologies are being created, who can predict possibilities for future professional development?

Guskey (2000) asserts that effective professional development follows the following four principles:

1. **Clear focus on learners:** Identifying clear goals in terms of student learning.

2. **Emphasis on individual and organizational change:** Clarifying reorganization of the school, such as scheduling and professional collaborative time, administrative roles in nurturing teachers through the change process, and new expectations for teachers.

3. **Small changes guided by vision:** Breaking down complex changes into incremental steps within the larger vision of a unified goal.

4. **Ongoing, embedded professional development:** Recognizing that professional development is not limited to an event, but rather is "an indispensable part of all forms of leadership and collegial sharing."

Evaluate and Adjust

At established benchmarks, the strategic planning team will evaluate progress with the initiative. They should examine data that measures the desired outcomes as well as related data that may reflect unintended consequences. Schools that want to keep stakeholders involved will share a summary of progress and any significant changes that are needed to the plan with faculty, families, and relevant community organizations.

In addition to evaluating progress of the change initiative as a whole, teachers should be encouraged to monitor and reflect on their own progress. According to Hutchens (2011), "people with a deep sense of personal mastery are on a lifelong journey of self discovery. They are keenly aware of the results they wish to create..., their current reality..., and the gap between those two states." This personal reflection encourages teachers to have a proactive rather than reactive approach to problem solving related to this initiative and their total professional practice.

During this stage, leaders will invite the strategic planning team to revisit the long-range picture by asking the question, "What would scale and sustainability look like?" If the initiative has begun as a small pilot, it's never too early to plant the seeds for the future. Stakeholders pause to envision implications for expanding across the whole school or serving as a model to others who will replicate the practices.

As the strategic planning team members consider how to expand, improve, and maintain the current initiative, they will also discuss the next problem to be addressed in the next round of the satisfaction cycle.

Celebrate Success

The core of burnout is lack of success on the job. Too often we move from one problem to the next without stopping to celebrate the progress we have made. Every initiative and every change has at least some degree of success, whether we achieved our intended outcomes or learned an important lesson along the way.

My husband has shared stories from his work in scientific research and development that include years of failed experiments before solutions were found. Scientists pause after each experiment to reflect and celebrate their learning. Maybe they learned that increased heat did not yield the results they hoped. They congratulate themselves that they are one step closer to figuring out the process. When they discover something that does work, they throw a party.

I can think of very few times that teachers celebrated what they had learned in the course of an initiative. After our year-long student challenge initiative, one high school threw a Happy Endings party where each team presented what they had learned about their challenge student. Some students made significant gains, but others resisted the team's efforts. All teams found important lessons they had learned. Most importantly, the principal congratulated the faculty for their commitment to finding ways to support the most challenging students.

Many schools hold award assemblies at the end of the year to recognize a few students who have earned recognition with grades, national test scores, and scholarship awards. Are they the only students who could be celebrated? Self-efficacy is based on self-recognition of achieving something that was a stretch and patting yourself on the back for a new accomplishment. Breakthroughs happen throughout the year for many students and faculty. You can't overdo celebrating moments of success.

The celebration needs to be sincere and meaningful. I remember that my son brought home a Student of the Week certificate soon after he transferred to a new school. When I asked why he wasn't excited about his award, he explained that all students who turned in all homework assignments got one. He wasn't fooled.

These celebrations don't have to be elaborate. The point is to make sure those who made the gains are acknowledged by others and pause a moment to acknowledge themselves. This applies to faculty who undertake changes in their practice, families who try new ways to support the school and their teenagers, and youths who strive to expand their learning capacity in new ways. How often does your school celebrate?

School transformation involves much more than writing a plan and putting it into action. School leaders who are knowledgeable about the change process, involve stakeholders early and often and foster a learning community culture. They support faculty to progress through the stages of the satisfaction cycle, including clarifying values and outcomes, identifying problems, exploring options, creating an action plan, implementing the plan, evaluating and adjusting, and celebrating success. These leaders are aware that each faculty member will travel on a personal journey throughout the initiative and will ensure that they have supports needed to implement sustained change.

EPILOGUE: STORIES OF POSSIBILITY

The greatest danger for most of us lies not in setting our aim too high and falling short; but in setting our aim too low and achieving our mark.

MICHELANGELO

Now that you have come this far into the book, you may be wondering about the possibilities that can be created from doing the work laid out here. Make no mistake about it—disrupting the status quo is a lot of work. Change creates uncertainty and discomfort for leaders, educators, families, and youth. So why bother? In the midst of massive systems change, we often forget that after all, our intent is about improving outcomes for individual students. I am reminded of an inspirational parable that is often shared at professional conferences.

The Starfish Story

A young man is walking along the ocean and sees a beach on which thousands and thousands of starfish have washed ashore. Further along he sees an old man, walking slowly and stooping often, picking up one starfish after another and tossing each one gently into the ocean.

"Why are you throwing starfish into the ocean?" he asks the old man.

"Because the sun is up and the tide is going out and if I don't throw them further in they will die."

"But, old man, don't you realize there are miles and miles of beach and starfish all along it! You can't possibly save them all, you can't even save one-tenth of them. In fact, even if you work all day, your efforts won't make any difference at all."

> The old man listened calmly and then bent down to pick up another starfish and threw it into the sea. "It made a difference to that one."
>
> Adapted from Loren Eiseley (1978), *The Star Thrower*

I will share three stories here that illustrate the possibilities for youth when caring adults step outside of routine-entrenched procedures and interact personally with the hidden possibilities of an individual student. The first story is about Mick, a persistent young man who used post-school supports to achieve his dream. The second is the story of Buddy, who was prevented from playing out his predetermined self-fulfilling script by an empowering school team. In the third story, Evan's future direction was altered by parents who learned about self-determination. All three have fictitious names and slightly altered details, but all three stories are based on real individuals and real events.

Mick

As Mick's transition coordinator, I interacted with him at several points throughout his years in middle and high school. He had an endearing appearance with a lopsided grin, hair standing up on one side, and one shirt tail perpetually untucked. I met with him, his teachers, and mother to share the results of his 8th grade vocational assessment. I had met with over 100 8th graders that year, but I recall that meeting. Mick's career interest was clear and specific—he wanted to be a medic. He was already volunteering at the local firehouse and shared glowing stories about supporting firefighters when they went on calls.

The problem was that Mick had a diagnosis of intellectual disability. At that time, before our current research on brain functioning, there was a universal agreement that learning for students with intellectual disabilities was limited. We used terms like plateau and ceiling to describe how much they could learn. At that point, Mick's reading and math assessments were five years below grade level. While he might make some more improvement, nobody believed that he would ever bring his reading up to the 10th grade level needed for medic school admission.

His teachers joked about his unrealistic dream of being a medic. They asked me to help him set a more attainable goal during our conference. But I never wanted to discourage my students from big dreams. I asked Mick why he wanted to be a medic. His explanation didn't sound like an unrealistic pipe dream like many who said they wanted to play for the NFL but had never tried out for a football team. He knew what it meant to be a medic. I was honest with him and told him that medic school required a 10th grade reading level.

During his senior year of high school, Mick only needed a few credits to graduate. There weren't many electives that he could pass, so he was scheduled for community work experience to complete his day. He would take English and social studies first thing in the morning, but unfortunately he needed to retake health during seventh period. Most of my work-study students were available by lunch time, but finding a part-time job to fit Mick's schedule would be challenging. Luckily, the chief custodian stopped me in the hall to say that he had funds to pay part-time students for cafeteria cleanup, and he asked, "Do you know anybody?"

Fortunately, Mick was willing, and it was a match. The custodian immediately took to Mick, but Mick's work ethic needed a lot of work. Between lunch shifts, he loved to race full speed down the length of the cafeteria with the wide push broom. Straw wrappers and his shirt tail fluttered in his wake. He learned that he could twirl the 50 gallon trashcans on the way to the dumpster, but he would not notice milk cartons that were scattered along the way. Suppressing my smile, I reminded him about the purpose of his job. Neither Mick nor I found another position that fit with his schedule, and he loved getting a school district paycheck. By the spring, both his supervisor and I had accepted that he would need to sweep the cafeteria floor multiple times before he was done. That was fine with him.

A year later, on lunch break from a transition meeting at our state rehabilitation center, I was in the cafeteria line, surprised to find Mick serving food. He grinned upon recognizing that I remembered him. How could I forget such a character? When I asked what he was doing here, he responded that his VR counselor said with his reading level, the only job he could get was in food service. He hated it and restated that he still wanted to be a medic. He punctuated his statement with a splat of mashed potatoes on my plate. Same old Mick. I moved down the line, pondering about our system that tried to fit square pegs into round holes.

I met Mick again two years later when I was taking a group of transition coordinators on a tour of the Single Step program at a local community college. This program was for students who wanted to improve their academic and efficacy skills during the single year after high school prior to entering college. It has since expanded to provide support and career preparation courses. Mick pulled me aside to proudly share that he would be giving a speech at his graduation next week. He wanted me to know that he had never forgotten my challenge to him. He had worked through this program to bring up his reading achievement score to a 10th grade level. The Single Step staff had worked with him on appropriate social behavior and grooming. I noticed that his shirt was tucked in and his hair was combed, but more importantly, I saw that Mick confidently looked at me with the eyes of someone who had found his way and gained self-respect. Further, he told me he had been accepted into medic school. He gave me credit, but it was his perseverance and his determination along with the community organizations that nurtured his potential rather than focus on his limitations. What if we did this for all our kids?

Buddy

I met Buddy when I worked as the resident inclusion consultant at a new vocational high school. We were conducting longitudinal research to investigate stakeholder perspectives on a new inclusive model. Teacher teams put an emphasis on wraparound support to empower students with disability awareness, personal responsibility for ownership of their learning, and requests for accommodations. He was one of four students we interviewed during the fall of his freshman year. At that time, although he had been in resource class for his middle school academics, he denied that he had a learning disability with attention deficit hyperactivity disorder. He shrugged and said prior teachers had called him lazy. It was probably true. Nobody in his family had graduated high school, and he didn't expect to be the first. In fact, he said he hated this school and couldn't wait to be 16 so he could drop out.

Mrs. Quinn, his special education learning support coach, got to work. She showed up in his classes and created organizers for complicated concepts so that content made more sense for Buddy. She broke projects into a list of steps and invited him to complete the first step. Each morning in homeroom—the one time each day that she met with her whole caseload—she offered to read aloud and extended time test accommodations to the whole group. She asked who wanted extra help on Mr. Brewer's research project. She gave students hints about how to meet expectations in different teachers' classrooms. She made herself available during lunch and after school for students who admitted that they needed help.

Mrs. Quinn told Buddy she wasn't going to care more about his success than he did. She was too busy with kids who wanted to succeed. But he had glimpses of other students who used her support and could then participate in class with their peers. He listened during homeroom when she shared stories of famous people who didn't let their disability stop them. He saw that teachers here understood that students used different approaches to learn, and didn't discourage them with hopeless labels of lazy and unmotivated. At report card time, Mrs. Quinn taught them how to calculate their GPAs and explained how to track their daily grades in the online system. Buddy began to see that the low grades were not a reflection of his teachers' opinions of him, but of his own work. When he completed an assignment well, he saw it improved his class average.

A turning point came for him with the IEP workshop in February. He had been a spectator at his IEP meetings since turning 14, but Mrs. Quinn explained that high school students get more responsibility for their own IEPs. They would host their IEP meetings this year and share with those on their team about their post-school goals. They discussed possible post-school goals, and Mrs. Quinn encouraged them to investigate college entrance requirements. She told them about the accommodations available in college and famous people with disabilities who had earned college degrees. Further, they would write at least one of their own IEP goals. She met with each of the 9th graders to help them identify one behavior or skill they wanted to work on that would improve their school success. They learned to write an IEP goal that was specific, measurable (with both their present and target levels), and listed the supports they thought they needed from adults, peers, or family.

Buddy had never been invited to set his own goals, but he decided to work on doing homework consistently for the first time in his life. When Mrs. Quinn asked what his big challenge would be, he said, "Remembering to bring stuff home, and making myself sit down to do it." So they developed some strategies that he could use. She congratulated him on taking the first step and acknowledged how difficult it is for everyone to make changes to their habitual behaviors. He made some progress, but it was easier for him to slide back into using the evenings as his own time.

As Buddy approached his 16th birthday, we held our breath. Would we lose him? All Buddy's teachers knew how hard life was for him outside of school. We knew that the chances were high that he would drop out. But he had started forming attachments with the guidance counselor, several of his teachers, and Mrs. Quinn. He led his IEP meeting and his courage to take ownership for his life was reinforced by the respect he earned from his team. He continued through the end of the year, barely passing his courses. He celebrated that there were no failing grades on his report card for the first time in his life.

Each year, surrounded by a network of adults who demonstrated that they believed in his potential, Buddy gradually developed resilient goal persistence. I interviewed him on the last day of his senior year. He told me, "If I had not come to this school, I'm sure I would have dropped out. Each year when I prepared to lead my IEP meeting, it reminded me to get back on track. I learned that it was up to me if I succeeded or not. I learned that teachers wouldn't know how to help me unless I told them what I needed. I'm grateful that I have learned I'm in charge of my life."

Evan

I met Evan when he presented his story at a national conference. I got acquainted over lunch with him and his mother, Carol, and his support network. Because he was diagnosed with autism and low intellectual functioning, he was sent at an early age to a school for students with developmental disabilities. At first, his mother was relieved because the teachers in this school reassured her that they had developed a system that guaranteed job placement upon graduation. Although few of their students would earn diplomas, they would learn life skills and how to use paratransit with support. Through partnerships with adult service agencies, all their students would become employed.

The year he turned 19, Evan participated in the work skills program with his fellow classmates. Evan rotated through several job skills stations. In his presentation he described his job at a food pantry distribution center. He was closely supervised by his job coach to ensure that he was following the correct procedures as he put one orange in each bag for two hours. Although he didn't express himself, Carol knew her son well enough to sense something was wrong. But when she talked to his teachers, she was told that he needed to learn to be a conscientious worker as this was the kind of work he would do for the rest of his life. His mother knew this school had a record of strong employment outcomes, but she started wondering if this was the best outcome for Evan.

At about this time, Carol received a call from Helen, Chuck's mother. The two boys had become friends when they attended the same special education preschool experiences years before. Helen was working on her master's degree in special education. She wondered if Evan would be willing to be her case study student for her transition course project. All parties agreed, and both Helen and Chuck showed up at Evan's house the next Saturday.

Helen explained that she would begin by asking Evan a list of questions called a transition assessment to learn more about what he wanted for his future. Evan was delighted to be the center of attention. Carol had never seen him so animated as he shared his opinions. She was surprised when he told Helen how bored he was with putting oranges into bags. She tried to remember the last time anyone asked her son for his opinion.

When Helen asked him about his favorite activities, he described the haunted hotel near his home that they visited repeatedly each fall. He started describing the various scenes in detail. He excitedly talked about the ghost that pops out of a closet, the scarecrow that suddenly flaps its arms, and the picture with a face that protrudes from the frame with a loud Boo! Chuck listened intently and asked questions about how they staged each scene.

Then Chuck spoke up. He told Evan that he needed to become a self-advocate. He needed to tell his teachers that he didn't want to put oranges into bags any more. He should tell them that he wanted a job at the haunted hotel. Everyone stared at Chuck in amazement. He continued, "I'm learning to tell my teachers about the accommodations I need to help me learn. You can do it, too."

That meeting was a turning point for Evan and the way his mother supported him, but now he had a peer mentor, too. At the second meeting Helen, Chuck, and Carol coached Evan for his upcoming second job interview at the haunted hotel. With their help, he understood that he wasn't hired at the first interview because he was too nervous to speak. He practiced answering questions that they posed to him. He did much better at the second interview and was hired to begin training right away.

There was a lot to learn—the scripts for the various scenes that he rotated through, how to apply his own makeup, and how to get along with coworkers who might not treat him nicely. But there was another problem. The haunted hotel was open from 6 pm until midnight on weekends. Sometimes it was late by the time the last guests left and everything was cleaned up. Carol didn't like driving late at night. Evan had heard about Uber and decided to try it. He now has his own account and learned how to use his phone to call an Uber driver, track its arrival, and pay from his account. Best of all, he pays for it with money he has earned doing work that he loves.

At Helen and Chuck's third visit, they helped Evan develop his PowerPoint profile. Using the slide show he created, Evan told his school IEP team about his weekend job at the haunted hotel, complete with pictures of himself in makeup and managing his own transportation. Carol sat by proudly and was pleased with the stunned look on the faces of his teachers.

Since that time, Evan has shared his PowerPoint profile with all the students and faculty at his school during a school assembly. He has spoken at state and national transition conferences with his mother smiling nearby. When he arrived at the national conference where I met him, he called for an Uber driver to meet them at the airport. Best of all, he convinced his team to place him in a comprehensive high school where he is pursuing career preparation in early childhood.

These three stories are just the beginning. Most teachers could tell you about students who achieved remarkable outcomes, but they aren't the norm *yet*. We need to collect stories of success and distribute them widely. Recognizing the importance of spreading news about the possibilities of high expectations, several organizations, such as PACER and IEL, have recently set up places on their websites to collect such stories. Those accounts inspire others to step up to foster a mindset to aim for high expectations for youth with disabilities. As in the starfish story, each of us has the possibility to make a difference one teacher, one parent, and one student at a time.

REFERENCES

Achieve. (2013). Closing the expectations gap. 2013 annual report on the alignment of state K-12 policies and practice with the demands of college and careers. Retrieved http://www.achieve.org/files/2013ClosingtheExpectationsGapReport.pdf

Baumeister R. F., & Tice, D.M. (2012). Cognitive, interpersonal, and behavioral effects of social exclusion: How people respond to rejection. In Aronson, J. & Aronson, E. (Eds). *Readings About the Social Animal.* (pp. 550-567) (11th ed). New York: Worth Publishers.

Blackorby, J., & Wagner, M. (1996). Longitudinal post-school outcomes of youth with disabilities: Findings from the national longitudinal transition study. *Exceptional Children, 62*(5), 399-414.

Blad, E. (2016, March 3). ESSA law broadens definition of school success. *Education Week*. Retrieved from http://www.edweek.org/ew/articles/2016/01/06/essa-law-broadens-definition-of-school-success.html

Blank, M.J., Melaville, A., & Shah, B.P. (2003, May). Making the difference: Research and practice in community schools. Coalition for Community Schools. Retrieved from http://www.communityschools.org/assets/1/Page/CCSFullReport.pdf

Brantlinger, E., Jimenez, R., Klingner, J., Pugach, M., & Richardson, V. (2005, January). Qualitative studies in special education. *Exceptional Children, 71,*195–207.

Bray, B., & McClaskey, K. (2014). *Make learning personal: The what, who, wow, where, and why.* Thousand Oaks, CA: Corwin Press.

Charles, C.M. (2002). *Essential elements of effective discipline.* Boston: Allyn & Bacon.

Coleman, A.L., Starzynski, A.L., Winnick, S.Y., Palmer, S.R., & Furr, J.E. (2006). *It takes a parent: Transforming education in the wake of the No Child Left Behind Act.* Washington, DC: Appleseed.

Cook, B.G., & Odom, S.L. (2013). Evidence-based practices and implementation science in special education. *Exceptional Children, 79*(2) 135-144.

Connect With Kids Network. (2016, February). Moving from tolerance to acceptance to understanding. *News and Trends.* Retrieved from http://connectwithkids.com/news-trends-february-2016

Coughlan, S. (2015, May 13). Asia tops biggest global school ratings. BBC. Retrieved from http://www.bbc.com/news/business-32608772

Covey, S.M.R. (2006). *The speed of trust: The one thing that changes everything.* New York: Free Press.

Cummings, C. (2000). *Winning strategies for classroom management.* Alexandria, VA: ASCD.

Dawson, P., & Guare, R. (2010). *Executive skills in children and adolescents: A practical guide to assessment and intervention.* (2nd ed). New York: Guilford Press.

Dean, C.B., Hubbell, E.R., Pitler, H. & Stone. B. (2012). *Classroom instruction that works: Research-based strategies for increasing student achievement.* (2nd ed). Alexandria, VA: ASCD.

DeBoer, A. (1995). *Working together: The art of consulting and communicating.* Longmont, CO: Sobris West.

Deci, E.L, & Ryan, R.M. (2002). The paradox of achievement: The harder you push, the worse it gets. In J. Aronson (Ed.), *Improving academic achievement: Impact of psychological factors on education* (pp. 62-84). San Diego, CA: Academic Press.

Dieker, L. (2007). *Demystifying secondary inclusion: Powerful school-wide and classroom strategies*. New York: Dude Publishing.

Dweck, C. (2006). *Mindset: The new psychology of success*. New York: Random House.

Eccles, M. P., & Mittman, B. S. (2006). Welcome to Implementation Science. *Implementation Science, 1*(1), 1–3. Retrieved from http://www.implementation science.com/content/1/1/1

Eisenman, L., Pleet, A. M., Wandry, D., & McGinley, V. (2010). Voices of special education teachers in an inclusive high school: Redefining responsibilities. *Remedial and Special Education. 32*(2), 91-104.

Entrepreneur Media. (2015). *Start your own business* (6th ed). Irvine, CA: Entrepreneur Media, Inc.

Epstein, J.L., Sanders, M.G., Sheldon, S. B., Simon, B.S., Salinas, K.C., Jansorn, N.R., et al. (2009). *School, family, and community partnerships: Your handbook for action* (3rd ed). Thousand Oaks, CA: Corwin Press.

Evans, R. (2015). *The human side of school change: Reform, resistance, and the real-life problems of innovation*. San Francisco: Jossey-Bass.

Fisher, R., & Brown, S. (1988). *Getting together: Building relationships as we negotiate*. New York: Penguin.

Friend, M., & Cook, L. (2000). *Interactions: Collaboration skills for school professionals*. New York: Longman.

Fullan, M. (2008). *The six secrets of change: What the best leaders do to help their organizations survive and thrive*. San Francisco: John Wiley & Sons.

Galinsky, E. (2010). *Mind in the making: The seven essential life skills every child needs*. New York: HarperCollins.

Gaskill, P.J., & Hoy, A. W., (2002). Self-efficacy and self-regulated learning: The dynamic duo in school performance. In Aronson, J. (Ed). *Improving Academic Achievement: Impact of Psychological Factors on Education.* (pp. 186-206). San Diego, CA: Academic Press.

Gately, S. E. (2005). Two are better than one. *Principal Leadership, 5*(9), 36-41.

Gersten, R., Fuchs, L.S., Compton, D., Coyne, M., Greenwood, C., & Innocenti, M.S. (2005, January). Quality indicators for group experimental and quasi-experimental research in special education. *Exceptional Children, 71,* 149-164.

Gore, M.C. (2010). *Inclusion strategies for secondary classrooms: Keys for struggling learners.* Thousand Oaks, CA: Corwin Press.

Guskey, T. R. (2000). *Evaluating professional development.* Thousand Oaks, CA: Corwin Press.

Harrist, A.W., & Bradley, K. D. (2002). Social exclusion in the classroom: Teachers and students as agents of change. In Aronson, J. (Ed). *Improving Academic Achievement: Impact of Psychological Factors on Education.* (pp. 364-382). San Diego, CA: Academic Press.

Henderson, A., Mapp, K., Johnson. V.R., & Davies, D. (2007). *Beyond the bake sale: The essential guide to family-school partnerships.* New York: The New Press.

Henley, M. (2006). *Classroom management: A proactive approach.* Upper Saddle River, NJ: Pearson Education.

Holcomb, S. (2016, Feb. 17). How one middle school cut discipline referrals by 98 percent in one year. *NEA Today.* Retrieved from http://neatoday. org/2016/02/17/middle-school-discipline-referrals/

Hollas, B. (2007). *Differentiating instruction in a whole-group setting: Taking the easy first steps into differentiation grades 7-12.* Peterborough, NH: Crystal Springs Books.

Horner, R.H., Carr, E.G, Halle, J., McGee, G., Odom, S. & Wolery, M. (2005, January). The use of single-subject research to identify evidence-based practice in special education. *Exceptional Children, 71,* 165-179.

Hutchens, D. (2011). *Outlearning the wolves: Surviving and thriving in a learning organization* (3rd ed). Waltham, MA: Pegasus Communications.

Innovative Schools Network. (n.d.) Innovation Zone Explained. Retrieved from http://innovativeschoolsnetwork.com/resources/pages/innoavation-zone-explained

Institute of Education Sciences National Center for Special Education Research. (2011). The post-high school outcomes of young adults with disabilities up to 8 years after high school: A report from the National Longitudinal Transition Study-2. Retrieved from http://www.nlts2.org/reports/2011_09_02/nlts2_report_2011_09_02_execsum.pdf

Kagan, S. (2013). *Kagan cooperative learning structures.* San Clemente, CA: Kagan Publishing.

King, J.B. (2016). *Supporting America's educators to expand opportunity.* Speech delivered in Philadelphia. Retrieved from http://www.ed.gov/news/speeches/supporting-americas-educators-expand-opportunity

Lhamon, C.E., Assistant Secretary for Civil Rights. (2014, October 21). Dear Colleague Letter: Responding to bullying of students with disabilities. Retrieved from http://www2.ed.gov/about/offices/list/ocr/letters/colleague-bullying-201410.pdf

Little, P. (2013). School-community learning partnerships: Essential to expanded learning success. In T. K. Peterson (Ed.), *Expanding minds and opportunities: leveraging the power of afterschool and summer learning for student success.* Washington, DC: Collaborative Communications Group.

Markova, D., & McArthur, A. (2015). *I am smart: A guide to recognizing and developing your child's natural strengths.* Park City, UT: SmartWired LLC.

Marzano, R.J., & Pickering, D.J. (2011). *The highly engaged classroom.* Bloomington, IN: Marzano Research Laboratory.

Meyer, A., Rose, D. H., & Gordon, D. (2014). *Universal design for learning: Theory and practice.* Wakefield, MA: CAST Professional Publishing.

Miller, R.L., Brickman, P, & Bolen, D. (2012). Attribution versus persuasion as a means for modifying behavior. In Aronson, J & Aronson, E. *Readings about the social animal.* (11th ed.). (pp.112-131). New York: Worth Publishers.

Murawski, W., & Dieker, L. (2013). *Leading the co-teaching dance: Leadership strategies to enhance team outcomes.* Arlington, VA: Council for Exceptional Children.

National Academy for Academic Leadership. (2016). Leadership and institutional change. Retrieved from http://www.thenationalacademy.org/ready/change.html#firstSecond

National Center on Response to Intervention. (2010, March). *Essential components of RTI: A closer look at response to intervention.* Washington, DC: U.S. Department of Education, Office of Special Education Programs, National Center on Response to Intervention.

National Secondary Transition Technical Assistance Center. (2012, May). NSTTAC Indicator 13 Checklist: Form B. Retrieved from http://www.transitionta.org/sites/default/files/transitionplanning/NSTTAC_ChecklistFormB.pdf

Neumann, J.W. (2013, Mar 19). Developing a new framework for conceptualizing "student-centered learning". *The Educational Forum, 77*(2), 161-175.

Odom, S.L., Brantlinger, E., Gersten, R., Horner, R.H., Thompson, B., & Harris, K.R. (2005). Research in special education: Scientific methods and evidence-based practices. *Exceptional Children, 71*(2), 137-148.

Overbaugh, R., & Schultz, L. (n.d.). Bloom's taxonomy revisited. Old Dominion University. Retrieved from https://www.uta.edu/ier/Resources/Blooms_Taxonomy_Revisited.pdf

PACER's National Bullying Prevention Center. (2016). Retrieved from http://www.pacer.org/bullying/about/media-kit/stats.asp

Panitz, T. (1999, Dec). Collaborative versus cooperative learning: A comparison of the two concepts which will help us understand the underlying nature of interactive learning. Retrieved from www.eric.ed.gov/contentdelivery/servlet/ERICServlet?accno=ED448443

Partnership for 21st Century Learning. (2015, May). P21 Framework definitions. Retrieved from http://www.p21.org/our-work/p21-framework

Positive Behavioral Supports and Interventions. (2016). Retrieved from https://www.pbis.org/school

Pugach, M.C., & Johnson, L.J. (2002). *Collaborative practitioners collaborative schools.* (2nd ed). Denver, CO: Love Publishing Company.

Randolph, K.A., & Johnson, J.L. (2008). School-based mentoring programs: A review of the research. *Children & Schools, 30*(3), 177-185.

Reeves, D. B. (2009). *Leading change in your school: How to conquer myths, build commitment, and get results.* Alexandria, VA: ASCD.

Rickabaugh, J. (2016). *Tapping the power of personalized learning: A roadmap for school leaders.* Alexandria, VA: ASCD.

Rose, T. (2013, June 19). The Myth of Average. TEDx Sonoma County. Retrieved from https://www.youtube.com/watch?v=4eBmyttcfU4

Rosenthal, R. (2002). The Pygmalion effect and its mediating mechanisms. In J. Aronson (Ed.), *Improving academic achievement: Impact of psychological factors on education* (pp.25-36). San Diego, CA: Academic Press.

Salend, S. J., & Duhaney, L. G. (1999). The impact of inclusion on students with and without disabilities and their educators. *Remedial & Special Education, 20*(2), 114-126.

Spiro, J. (2009). Leading change handbook: Concepts and tools. Retrieved from www.wallacefoundation.org

Stark, P., & Noel, A.M. (2015). Trends in high school dropout and completion rates in the United States: 1972–2012 (NCES 2015). U.S. Department of Education. Washington, DC: National Center for Education Statistics.

Stoddard, S. (2014). 2014 disability statistics annual report. Durham, NH: University of New Hampshire.

Thompson, B., Diamond, K.E., McWilliam, R., Snyder, P. & Snyder, S.W. (2005, January). Evaluating the quality of evidence from correlational research for evidence-based practice. *Exceptional Children, 71*, 181-194.

U.S. Department of Education (2015a) Draft policy statement on family engagement from the early years to the early grades. Retrieved from https://www.acf.hhs.gov/sites/default/files/ecd/draft_hhs_ed_family_engagement.pdf

U.S. Department of Education (2015b). IDEA section 618 data products: Static tables. Retrieved from http://www2.ed.gov/programs/osepidea/618-data/static-tables/index.html#part-b

U.S. Department of Education, Comprehensive Centers Program. (n.d.) Retrieved from http://www2.ed.gov/programs/newccp/index.html

U.S. Department of Special Education Policy (2012, May). Results-driven accountability in special education summary 4-5-12. Retrieved from https://www2.ed.gov/about/offices/list/osers/osep/rda-summary.pdf

Villa, R.A., Thousand, J.S., & Nevin, A.I. (2008). *A guide to co-teaching: Practical tips for facilitating student learning* (2nd ed.). Thousand Oaks, CA: Corwin Press.

Wachtel, K. (2011, June 13). The 13 most common reasons you're likely to get fired. *Business Insider*. Retrieved from http://www.businessinsider.com/the-13-most-common-reasons-why-employees-get-fired-2011-6

Wehmeyer, M.L., Field, S., & Thoma, C.A. (2012). Self-determination and adolescent transition education. In Wehmeyer, M.L. & Webb, K.W. (Eds). *Handbook of Adolescent Transition Education for Youth with Disabilities.* New York: Routledge.

Wilson, T.D., Damiani, M., & Shelton, N. (2002). Improving the academic performance of college students with brief attributional interventions. In J. Aronson (Ed.), *Improving academic achievement: Impact of psychological factors on education* (pp. 91-107). San Diego, CA: Academic Press.

ABOUT THE AUTHOR

Amy M. Pleet-Odle, Ed.D. has nearly five decades of experience in education as an English teacher, special education teacher/ department chair, and transition coordinator at the local school, district, and state levels. She was responsible for special education teacher preparation and effectiveness as the Special Education Graduate Director/ Associate Professor at Towson University and subsequently Secondary Inclusion Consultant at University of Delaware. Her publications provide a framework for improving teachers' effectiveness in working with families and empowering youth. Her consulting company, Inclusion Focused Coaching, provides professional development and technical assistance in school transformation, especially targeting effectiveness of special education services, administrative role, family engagement, and youth empowerment. As a parent of young adults with disabilities, she awakens professional sensitivity to parent perspectives.

Made in USA - Kendallville, IN
45839_9781535564519
12.14.2023 1440